Software QA Engineer

An Advanced Handbook for Intermediate Professionals

Steven Dent

Table Of Contents

Introduction

Quality assurance (QA) in software engineering stands as a critical pillar in the development lifecycle, ensuring that software products meet the rigorous standards expected by users and stakeholders. As technology advances, the role of the Software QA Engineer has become increasingly complex and essential, requiring a nuanced understanding of both technical and managerial aspects. This handbook is designed for intermediate professionals looking to deepen their expertise and advance their careers in software quality assurance.

In recent years, software development methodologies have evolved significantly, driven by the need for faster delivery cycles, more reliable applications, and enhanced user experiences. Agile and DevOps practices, for instance, have transformed how teams collaborate, integrate, and deliver software. These methodologies emphasize continuous testing and integration, positioning QA engineers not just as gatekeepers but as integral participants in the development process. Understanding and navigating these methodologies is crucial for any QA professional aiming to stay relevant and effective.

As we delve into the complexities of modern QA practices, it's essential to recognize the diverse skill set required of today's QA engineers. Beyond the traditional tasks of identifying and documenting bugs, QA engineers now engage in designing and implementing automated test frameworks, performing security assessments, and ensuring compliance with various standards and regulations. They are expected to have a strong grasp of programming languages, testing tools, and frameworks, along with soft skills such as communication, problem-solving, and teamwork.

This handbook aims to provide a comprehensive guide to mastering these skills, offering insights into advanced techniques and best practices. We begin with an exploration of the current landscape of software development, examining how QA fits into various development methodologies. This foundation is crucial, as it sets the stage for understanding the strategic role of QA in delivering high-quality software.

Next, we delve into the technical competencies required of a modern QA engineer. Automated testing, a cornerstone of contemporary QA practices, is covered extensively. We explore various automation tools and frameworks, discussing their applications, benefits, and limitations. The focus is on practical implementation, providing readers with the knowledge to design, develop, and maintain effective automated test suites.

Security testing is another critical area we address, reflecting the growing importance of cybersecurity in today's digital environment. This section covers techniques for identifying vulnerabilities and ensuring that software products are resilient against attacks. We also discuss compliance testing, highlighting the importance of adhering to industry standards and regulations, which is increasingly becoming a significant aspect of the QA role.

Performance testing is examined in detail, offering strategies to evaluate the responsiveness, stability, and scalability of applications under various conditions. This section provides insights into the tools and techniques used to simulate different load scenarios, identify bottlenecks, and optimize performance.

In addition to technical skills, we emphasize the importance of soft skills in QA engineering. Effective communication, both within the QA team and with other stakeholders, is crucial for success. We explore strategies for fostering collaboration, managing conflicts, and ensuring that QA processes are well-integrated into the broader development workflow.

The handbook also addresses the career development of QA professionals. We provide guidance on building a professional portfolio, pursuing certifications, and staying updated with industry trends and emerging technologies. The goal is to equip readers with the tools and knowledge to advance their careers and contribute meaningfully to their organizations.

Finally, we offer case studies and real-world examples to illustrate the concepts discussed throughout the book. These practical examples provide context and demonstrate how advanced QA techniques are applied in real software development projects. By examining these case studies, readers can gain a deeper understanding of the challenges and solutions encountered in the QA process.

In conclusion, this handbook serves as a valuable resource for intermediate QA professionals seeking to enhance their skills and advance their careers. By providing a comprehensive overview of modern QA practices and offering practical insights and examples, we aim to empower readers to become more effective and impactful in their roles. The journey to mastering software quality assurance is continuous, and this book is intended to be a guide and companion on that path.

Chapter One

Advanced Test Design Techniques

Equivalence Partitioning

Equivalence Partitioning (EP) stands as one of the foundational techniques in software test design, streamlining the process of crafting test cases that effectively capture potential defects. As QA engineers seek to optimize test coverage while minimizing redundancy, understanding and applying EP becomes crucial. This technique enables testers to categorize input data into equivalence classes, each representing a subset of inputs that are expected to elicit similar behavior from the system under test.

Concept and Rationale

At its core, Equivalence Partitioning involves dividing the input data into partitions or classes. Each partition, known as an equivalence class, is designed to represent a set of inputs that should be treated identically by the software. The primary rationale is that if a particular input within a class triggers a specific behavior or response, then all other inputs within the same class should elicit the same response. Conversely, if a defect is found using one input from a class, similar defects are likely to be found using other inputs from the same class.

This technique reduces the number of test cases required to achieve comprehensive test coverage, as it enables testers to focus on representative values from each class rather than exhaustively testing all possible inputs. By doing so, testers can detect defects more efficiently and ensure that the software behaves correctly across a wide range of inputs.

Steps to Implement Equivalence Partitioning

Implementing Equivalence Partitioning involves a structured approach that can be broken down into several key steps:

1. **Identify the input domain**: Begin by identifying the range of valid and invalid inputs for the system. This includes all possible inputs that the system can accept and the conditions under which these inputs are considered valid or invalid.

2. **Divide the input domain into equivalence classes**: Categorize the inputs into equivalence classes. Each class should group inputs that are expected to produce the same result or response from the system. There are typically two types of equivalence classes:

    - **Valid equivalence classes**: These represent inputs that are within the acceptable range or meet the specified criteria.

    - **Invalid equivalence classes**: These represent inputs that fall outside the acceptable range or do not meet the specified criteria.

3. **Select representative values**: For each equivalence class, choose one or more representative values to be used in testing. These values should be selected based on their ability to effectively represent the entire class.

4. **Design test cases**: Create test cases using the representative values selected in the previous step. Each test case should be designed to verify that the system handles the inputs correctly, both for valid and invalid classes.

5. **Execute and evaluate**: Run the test cases and evaluate the results. If a defect is found using a particular input, it is likely that other inputs within the same equivalence class will also cause similar issues.

Practical Application

To illustrate the practical application of Equivalence Partitioning, consider a software system that accepts numerical inputs ranging from 1 to 100. The goal is to ensure that the system correctly processes these inputs.

1. **Identify the input domain**: The valid input range is 1 to 100. Inputs outside this range are considered invalid.

2. **Divide the input domain into equivalence classes**:

   - Valid equivalence classes: [1-50], [51-100]

   - Invalid equivalence classes: Less than 1, Greater than 100

3. **Select representative values**:

   - For the valid equivalence class [1-50], select 25.

- For the valid equivalence class [51-100], select 75.
- For the invalid equivalence class less than 1, select -1.
- For the invalid equivalence class greater than 100, select 101.

4. **Design test cases**:
   - Test case 1: Input = 25 (expected: valid input, processed correctly)
   - Test case 2: Input = 75 (expected: valid input, processed correctly)
   - Test case 3: Input = -1 (expected: invalid input, error message or rejection)
   - Test case 4: Input = 101 (expected: invalid input, error message or rejection)
5. **Execute and evaluate**: Run the test cases and verify that the system handles each input as expected. If an error is detected for input 25, similar errors might be expected for other values in the [1-50] range.

Benefits of Equivalence Partitioning

Equivalence Partitioning offers several benefits that make it a valuable technique in the software testing arsenal:

1. **Efficiency**: By reducing the number of test cases required to cover a wide range of inputs, EP enhances

testing efficiency. Testers can achieve comprehensive coverage without the need to test every possible input individually.

2. **Focus**: EP allows testers to focus on representative values that are more likely to uncover defects. This targeted approach increases the likelihood of identifying critical issues.

3. **Scalability**: EP is highly scalable and can be applied to complex systems with large input domains. By categorizing inputs into manageable classes, testers can effectively manage and test extensive input ranges.

4. **Defect Detection**: EP helps in identifying defects that might be overlooked with random testing. By systematically covering all equivalence classes, testers ensure that all potential behaviors are evaluated.

Challenges and Considerations

While Equivalence Partitioning is a powerful technique, it is not without its challenges and considerations:

1. **Class Definition**: Defining equivalence classes requires a deep understanding of the system under test and its expected behavior. Incorrectly defined classes can lead to inadequate test coverage or false positives/negatives.

2. **Complex Inputs**: For systems with complex input structures, such as multi-dimensional inputs or interdependent parameters, defining equivalence

classes can be more challenging. Testers must consider all relevant factors to ensure comprehensive coverage.

3. **Boundary Values**: While EP focuses on representative values within each class, boundary values also play a critical role in testing. Combining EP with Boundary Value Analysis (BVA) can enhance test coverage by addressing potential edge cases.

4. **Maintenance**: As the system evolves, equivalence classes may need to be redefined to reflect changes in input requirements or behavior. Maintaining and updating equivalence classes is essential to ensure ongoing test effectiveness.

Integrating EP with Other Techniques

To maximize its effectiveness, Equivalence Partitioning is often integrated with other test design techniques. One common combination is with Boundary Value Analysis (BVA), which focuses on testing the boundaries between equivalence classes. By combining EP with BVA, testers can ensure that both representative values and boundary conditions are thoroughly evaluated.

Another complementary technique is Decision Table Testing, which helps in capturing complex input combinations and their expected outcomes. Integrating EP with Decision Table Testing allows for a more comprehensive analysis of how different inputs interact and affect the system's behavior.

Equivalence Partitioning is a fundamental technique in the advanced test design toolkit of a QA engineer. By systematically categorizing inputs into equivalence classes and focusing on representative values, EP enables efficient and effective testing. While it presents challenges, particularly in defining classes and handling complex inputs, the benefits of improved efficiency, scalability, and defect detection make it indispensable. Integrating EP with other techniques further enhances its utility, ensuring that all potential input scenarios are rigorously tested. As software systems continue to grow in complexity, mastering Equivalence Partitioning will remain essential for delivering high-quality, reliable software.

Boundary Value Analysis

Boundary Value Analysis (BVA) stands as a cornerstone technique in the toolkit of Software QA Engineers. It zeroes in on the peripheries of input values, pinpointing vulnerabilities that often lurk at these critical junctures. This methodology hinges on the premise that errors are most prone to manifest at the extremities of input ranges, where software behavior may diverge unpredictably.

Unpacking Boundary Value Analysis

BVA operates under the straightforward principle that issues are more likely to surface at the boundaries of input ranges. This occurs because these points represent transitions or shifts in conditions, which can expose flaws in the underlying code. For example, if a system accepts input values ranging from 1 to 100, BVA would scrutinize values like 1, 100, and those immediately adjacent (e.g., 0 and 101).

The rationale behind BVA is clear-cut: developers frequently overlook edge cases, making boundary values fertile ground for defects. By focusing testing efforts on these critical junctures, QA engineers increase the likelihood of identifying issues that may remain hidden during testing of non-boundary values.

Implementing Boundary Value Analysis

Implementing BVA effectively involves several key steps, beginning with identifying the boundaries of the input range and then crafting test cases that scrutinize values precisely at, just below, and just above these boundaries:

1. **Define the Input Range**: Establish the permissible range of input values, drawing from specifications, design documents, or consultations with stakeholders.

2. **Identify Critical Boundaries**: Once the input range is defined, pinpoint the critical boundary values. These include the minimum and maximum values of the range, as well as values immediately outside this range.

3. **Construct Test Cases**: Develop test cases that encompass these boundary values. For each identified boundary, generate tests that encompass:

    - The boundary value itself

    - Values immediately below the boundary

    - Values immediately above the boundary

For instance, consider a software application that processes age inputs ranging from 18 to 60. The boundary values in this case would be 18 and 60. Therefore, the test suite would encompass values like 17, 18, 19, 59, 60, and 61.

Practical Considerations in BVA

While BVA's underlying concept is intuitive, its application can pose challenges. Input ranges in real-world scenarios often involve multiple dimensions, necessitating the identification and testing of boundaries across several parameters simultaneously. This complexity enriches the testing process but also demands greater rigor in test case design.

1. **Single vs. Multiple Boundaries**: In simpler cases involving single variables, applying BVA is relatively straightforward. However, many applications require testing across multiple input parameters, each with its own set of boundaries. For instance, an application form capturing both age (18-60) and income ($30,000-$120,000) necessitates multi-dimensional boundary testing.

2. **Interdependent Boundaries**: Boundaries are often interconnected rather than standalone. For example, certain combinations of age and income might trigger errors even if each parameter individually falls within its respective range. BVA must accommodate these interdependencies, crafting test cases that explore how boundaries intersect across multiple inputs.

3. **Handling Non-Numeric Boundaries**: Although BVA is typically associated with numeric inputs, its

principles can extend to non-numeric domains such as string lengths or date ranges. For instance, validating a text field with a maximum length of 255 characters would involve testing string lengths of 254, 255, and 256 characters.

Advantages of BVA

BVA offers significant advantages in software testing. By targeting boundary values, QA engineers can uncover a broad spectrum of defects with a modest number of test cases. This efficiency renders BVA particularly attractive in scenarios where time and resources are constrained.

1. **Efficiency**: BVA optimizes testing efforts by zeroing in on the most vulnerable areas of the input space. This allows for comprehensive testing without the need for an exhaustive number of test scenarios.

2. **Effectiveness**: Boundary values are notorious for exposing defects. By concentrating testing on these pivotal points, BVA enhances the likelihood of detecting faults that could potentially disrupt software functionality in real-world usage.

3. **Simplicity**: The application of BVA is straightforward and accessible to QA professionals at various skill levels, contributing to its widespread adoption in testing practices.

Limitations of BVA

Despite its strengths, BVA has limitations that necessitate careful consideration. While effective for detecting boundary-related defects, BVA alone may not suffice for identifying issues within the middle of input ranges or for uncovering complex interactions between multiple inputs.

1. **Incomplete Coverage**: BVA's focus on boundaries may inadvertently overlook defects that arise within the input range. Supplementary testing techniques such as equivalence partitioning are often required to ensure comprehensive test coverage.

2. **Assumption of Linear Boundaries**: BVA is most effective when input domains exhibit clear, linear boundaries. In cases where boundaries are convoluted or non-linear, BVA's efficacy may diminish.

3. **Dependency on Input Domain Knowledge**: Successful application of BVA hinges on a thorough understanding of the input range and its boundaries. Ambiguous or incomplete specifications can impede the accurate implementation of BVA.

Integrating BVA with Other Techniques

To mitigate its limitations, BVA is frequently integrated with complementary test design techniques. Combining BVA with methods such as equivalence partitioning, decision table testing, and state transition testing can augment test coverage and fortify the overall testing strategy.

1. **Equivalence Partitioning**: This technique categorizes the input domain into equivalence classes, each representing a group of inputs expected to elicit similar software behavior. By intertwining BVA with equivalence partitioning, QA engineers ensure

comprehensive testing across both boundary and non-boundary values.

2. **Decision Table Testing**: Decision tables excel in scenarios where software behavior hinges on various combinations of input conditions. By amalgamating BVA with decision table testing, QA engineers scrutinize how different input combinations influence boundary conditions.

3. **State Transition Testing**: For systems governed by sequential input states, state transition testing proves invaluable. Integrating BVA with state transition testing enables QA engineers to probe how boundary conditions manifest across different application states.

Case Study: Real-World Application of BVA

Consider an online retail platform that manages customer orders. The platform stipulates that order quantities must fall between 1 and 100 units. Additionally, orders can only proceed if sufficient stock is available, defined as at least 10 units.

1. **Identify Boundaries**: The critical boundaries in this scenario are 1 and 100 for order quantities, and 10 units for stock availability.

2. **Develop Test Cases**:

    - Order quantities: 0 (just below minimum), 1 (minimum), 2 (just above minimum), 99 (just below maximum), 100 (maximum), 101 (just above maximum)

- Stock availability: 9 (just below required minimum), 10 (minimum required), 11 (just above minimum required)

Through rigorous application of BVA, QA teams ensure the platform's ability to handle order scenarios precisely at these pivotal points. Additional test cases could explore combinations of these boundaries, such as placing an order for 1 unit when stock availability is exactly 10 units.

Boundary Value Analysis emerges as a potent technique for unearthing defects that often manifest at the fringes of input ranges. By scrutinizing boundary values, QA engineers optimize the efficacy and efficiency of their testing endeavors. While BVA possesses inherent limitations, its integration with complementary test design techniques bolsters overall test coverage and enhances software reliability. Ultimately, mastering BVA equips QA professionals with a critical toolset for delivering robust, high-quality software that meets user expectations.

Decision Table Testing

The pursuit of effective testing methodologies remains crucial in the realm of software quality assurance. Among these methodologies, Decision Table Testing stands out as a sophisticated technique utilized by experienced QA engineers to ensure thorough testing and validation of software systems. Built on logical constructs and systematic analysis, Decision Table Testing offers a structured approach to testing that enhances the reliability and accuracy of software applications.

Understanding Decision Table Testing

Decision Table Testing is a methodical approach to functional testing where test cases are designed based on combinations of inputs and their corresponding outputs. It is particularly effective in scenarios where the behavior of the system depends on various input conditions and rules. By systematically organizing inputs, actions, and expected outcomes into a tabular format, QA engineers can methodically verify the correctness of the software under different conditions.

The core components of a Decision Table typically include:

- **Conditions:** These represent the inputs or circumstances that influence the behavior of the software.
- **Actions:** These denote the operations or behaviors that the software should exhibit based on the input conditions.
- **Rules:** These define the relationships between conditions and actions, outlining the decision-making logic of the system.

Advantages of Decision Table Testing

1. Comprehensive Coverage:

Decision Table Testing ensures thorough coverage of various scenarios and combinations of inputs. By systematically exploring different conditions and their permutations, QA engineers can identify edge cases and unexpected behaviors that might not be apparent through other testing methods.

2. Clarity and Transparency:

The tabular representation of Decision Tables enhances clarity and simplifies the understanding of complex decision-making processes within the software. This clarity aids not only in testing but also in communication among team members regarding the expected behaviors of the system.

3. Efficient Bug Detection:

Due to its structured approach, Decision Table Testing facilitates early detection of defects and inconsistencies in the software logic. By systematically testing all possible combinations of conditions, QA engineers can pinpoint specific conditions or rules that may lead to failures or undesired outcomes.

4. Reusable and Maintainable:

Decision Tables can be reused across different phases of the software development lifecycle. Once created, they serve as valuable artifacts that can be updated and maintained as the software evolves. This reusability reduces redundancy in testing efforts and ensures consistency in test coverage over time.

Implementing Decision Table Testing

Step-by-Step Approach:

1. **Identify Conditions and Actions:** Begin by thoroughly understanding the functional requirements of the software. Identify all possible conditions (input variables) that influence the behavior of the system and define the corresponding actions or outputs.

2. **Create the Decision Table:** Construct a decision table by listing all identified conditions as columns and their possible combinations as rows. Each cell in the table represents a specific scenario defined by the combination of conditions and the expected action or outcome.

3. **Define Rules:** Populate the decision table with rules that specify the relationship between conditions and actions. These rules articulate the decision logic that the software must follow under different circumstances.

4. **Generate Test Cases:** Derive test cases from the decision table by selecting representative combinations of conditions. Each test case should cover a unique set of conditions and verify the corresponding actions or outcomes predicted by the decision table.

5. **Execute and Validate:** Execute the generated test cases against the software and compare the actual outcomes with those predicted by the decision table. Validate whether the software behaves as expected under different input conditions and whether it adheres to the defined decision rules.

Case Study: Application in Real-World Scenarios

To illustrate the practical application of Decision Table Testing, consider a banking application that processes loan applications. The decision to approve or reject a loan is influenced by multiple factors such as credit score, income level, and loan amount. By constructing a decision table encompassing these conditions and their corresponding approval criteria, QA engineers can systematically validate the decision-making logic of the application.

In this scenario:

- **Conditions** might include ranges of credit scores, income levels, and loan amounts.
- **Actions** could be approval or rejection of the loan application.
- **Rules** would define the specific thresholds and criteria for approving or rejecting loans based on combinations of these conditions.

By systematically testing various combinations of credit scores, income levels, and loan amounts using Decision Table Testing, QA engineers can ensure that the banking application makes accurate and consistent decisions across different scenarios.

Challenges and Considerations

While Decision Table Testing offers significant advantages, it is not without challenges:

- **Complexity Management:** As the number of conditions and rules increases, decision tables can become complex and difficult to manage.

- **Maintenance Overhead:** Updating decision tables to reflect changes in requirements or business rules requires careful coordination and may necessitate revisiting existing test cases.

- **Skill Requirements:** Designing effective decision tables demands a thorough understanding of the software's logic and the ability to translate complex business rules into a structured format.

Decision Table Testing stands as a powerful tool in the arsenal of QA engineers, enabling them to systematically validate software functionality across a spectrum of conditions and inputs. By leveraging its structured approach and logical framework, QA teams can enhance test coverage, improve defect detection, and ensure the reliability and accuracy of software systems. As software development continues to evolve, Decision Table Testing remains a cornerstone technique for achieving robust quality assurance in the dynamic world of technology.

In essence, Decision Table Testing exemplifies the meticulous craftsmanship required in advanced test design techniques, offering a structured pathway towards software quality excellence.

State Transition Testing

In the realm of software quality assurance (QA), where precision and effectiveness are paramount, advanced test design techniques play a pivotal role in ensuring robust software applications. Among these techniques, State Transition Testing stands out as a methodical approach to validating software behavior under various states and transitions. This technique is particularly valuable for intermediate professionals looking to deepen their understanding and proficiency in software testing.

Understanding State Transition Testing

At its core, State Transition Testing focuses on the different states a system can be in and the transitions between these states triggered by certain events. These states and transitions are often critical to the functionality and integrity of the software being tested. Consider a scenario where a system behaves differently depending on its current state—a classic example being a vending machine that changes behavior based on whether it is idle, dispensing a product, or out of stock.

In software terms, these states can represent anything from user interface modes (such as login, logged-in, and logged-out) to complex backend processes (like database synchronization states or transaction stages). The transitions, on the other hand, denote the actions or events that cause the system to move from one state to another—a button click, a database update, or an external trigger, for instance.

Principles of State Transition Testing

The essence of State Transition Testing lies in systematically defining and testing these states and transitions. Here's a structured approach to employing this technique effectively:

1. **Identifying States**: Begin by identifying all possible states the system can assume during its operation. This involves a thorough analysis of the software's specifications, user interactions, and system responses. Each state should be clearly defined and understood in terms of its inputs, outputs, and conditions.

2. **Mapping Transitions**: Once the states are identified, map out the transitions between these states. Document the events or actions that cause each transition and the resulting state change. This mapping helps in creating a comprehensive test coverage that ensures all possible state transitions are validated.

3. **Designing Test Cases**: With states and transitions mapped, design test cases that cover different scenarios. Test cases should encompass valid transitions, invalid transitions (where applicable), and boundary conditions. Consider edge cases where unexpected inputs or sequences of events might occur.

4. **Executing Tests**: Implement the designed test cases and execute them systematically. During execution, observe how the system transitions between states and validate that the transitions occur as expected. Log any discrepancies or deviations from expected behavior for further analysis.

5. **Analyzing Results**: Analyze test results to identify any defects or inconsistencies in state transitions. This analysis is crucial for debugging and refining the software, ensuring that it operates reliably under various conditions.

Advantages of State Transition Testing

State Transition Testing offers several distinct advantages, making it a preferred technique in the arsenal of QA professionals:

- **Coverage**: By focusing on states and transitions, this technique provides comprehensive test coverage, ensuring that all critical system behaviors are validated.

- **Efficiency**: Test cases derived from state transition diagrams are often efficient in uncovering defects related to state management and transitions.

- **Clarity**: The visual nature of state transition diagrams aids in clear communication and understanding among stakeholders, including developers, testers, and project managers.

- **Early Detection**: Issues related to state handling and transitions can be identified early in the development lifecycle, reducing the cost and effort of fixing defects in later stages.

Challenges and Considerations

While powerful, State Transition Testing does present challenges that practitioners should be aware of:

- **Complexity**: Systems with numerous states and intricate transitions can lead to complex diagrams and extensive test cases.

- **Maintenance**: As software evolves, state transitions may change, requiring test cases to be updated accordingly.

- **Combination Explosion**: Testing all possible combinations of states and transitions can be impractical in large systems, necessitating prioritization based on risk and criticality.

Practical Application in Software QA

To illustrate the practical application of State Transition Testing, consider a web application designed for online shopping. The application has various states such as browsing, adding items to cart, proceeding to checkout, payment processing, and order confirmation. Transitions between these states occur based on user actions (clicks, form submissions) and system responses (validation errors, payment failures).

By employing State Transition Testing, QA engineers can systematically validate:

- **Correct State Handling**: Ensure the application behaves appropriately in each defined state, displaying relevant information and options to the user.

- **Smooth Transitions**: Verify that transitions between states are seamless, with appropriate feedback provided to the user at each step.

- **Exception Handling**: Test how the application responds to unexpected events during state transitions, such as network errors or session timeouts.

In conclusion, State Transition Testing stands as a cornerstone technique for intermediate software QA professionals aiming to enhance their testing strategies. By focusing on the discrete states a system can assume and the transitions between them, this method ensures thorough validation of software behavior across various scenarios. Its structured approach not only improves test coverage but also facilitates early defect detection, contributing to the overall quality and reliability of software applications. As software systems continue to grow in complexity, mastering advanced test design techniques like State Transition Testing becomes increasingly indispensable for ensuring software meets its functional requirements with precision and robustness.

Chapter Two

Advanced Test Automation Strategies

Test Automation Design Patterns

The role of test automation has become increasingly crucial. As organizations strive for faster delivery cycles without compromising on quality, the adoption of advanced test automation strategies has emerged as a critical component in achieving these goals. At the heart of these strategies lie Test Automation Design Patterns, which serve as proven solutions to common automation challenges faced by intermediate professionals in the industry.

Understanding Test Automation Design Patterns

Test Automation Design Patterns can be likened to reusable blueprints or templates that encapsulate best practices and solutions to recurring automation problems. They provide a structured approach to designing automated tests, enhancing the maintainability, scalability, and reliability of the overall test suite. For the intermediate software QA engineer, familiarity with these patterns not only streamlines the automation process but also elevates the quality of test cases and reduces the effort required for maintenance.

Key Benefits of Test Automation Design Patterns

One of the primary advantages of leveraging Test Automation Design Patterns is their ability to promote consistency across automated test suites. By adhering to established patterns, QA engineers ensure that tests are structured uniformly, making them easier to understand and modify as the application evolves. This consistency also fosters collaboration among team members, as everyone follows a standardized approach to automation.

Moreover, Test Automation Design Patterns enhance the maintainability of automated tests. As software applications undergo changes over time, automated tests must be updated accordingly to ensure they remain effective. Design patterns provide a framework that anticipates such changes, making it simpler to adapt tests to new requirements or modifications in the application under test. This proactive approach reduces the likelihood of test failures due to outdated automation scripts, thereby contributing to overall testing efficiency.

Another significant benefit of these patterns is their role in improving the scalability of test automation efforts. As projects expand in scope or complexity, QA engineers often need to extend existing test suites or integrate new tests seamlessly. Design patterns offer scalable solutions that accommodate growth without compromising the integrity of the automation framework. This scalability is particularly crucial in agile and DevOps environments where rapid iterations and continuous integration demand robust, adaptable automation strategies.

Common Test Automation Design Patterns

There are several well-established Test Automation Design Patterns that address various aspects of test automation:

1. **Page Object Model (POM):** Perhaps the most widely recognized pattern, POM separates the logical structure

of a web page from the automation scripts that interact with it. By encapsulating page-specific behaviors and elements within dedicated classes or objects, POM promotes reusability and enhances the maintainability of UI tests.

2. **Factory Pattern:** This pattern focuses on creating objects without specifying the exact class of object that will be created. In test automation, the Factory Pattern can be employed to instantiate different types of test objects based on runtime conditions or configurations, facilitating dynamic test case creation and execution.

3. **Data-Driven Testing:** Involves separating test input data from test scripts, allowing QA engineers to execute the same test logic with multiple datasets. This pattern enhances test coverage and ensures that automated tests validate application behavior across various scenarios, improving overall test effectiveness.

4. **Behavior-Driven Development (BDD):** While not exclusive to test automation, BDD principles and frameworks like Cucumber or SpecFlow enable collaboration between QA engineers, developers, and domain experts. BDD encourages writing executable specifications in natural language format, translating business requirements into automated test scenarios that verify application functionality.

5. **Decorator Pattern:** This pattern allows behavior to be added to individual objects, dynamically, without affecting the behavior of other objects from the same class. In test automation, decorators can be used to extend the functionality of test cases without modifying

their underlying structure, promoting code reuse and enhancing flexibility in test design.

Implementing Test Automation Design Patterns

Implementing Test Automation Design Patterns effectively requires a deep understanding of both the application under test and the specific automation challenges being addressed. Intermediate professionals in software QA can benefit from studying real-world implementations of these patterns across different projects and industries. This exposure not only reinforces theoretical knowledge but also cultivates practical insights into adapting patterns to diverse testing scenarios.

Furthermore, the choice of which patterns to apply depends on factors such as project requirements, team expertise, and the nature of the application. For instance, complex web applications might benefit significantly from the Page Object Model, whereas data-intensive systems could leverage Data-Driven Testing to validate various input scenarios efficiently.

Successful implementation also hinges on selecting appropriate tools and frameworks that support the chosen design patterns. For example, tools like Selenium WebDriver are well-suited for implementing the Page Object Model due to their support for interacting with web elements in a structured manner. Similarly, integrating BDD frameworks requires selecting tools that align with the team's preferred programming language and development environment.

Challenges and Considerations

While Test Automation Design Patterns offer numerous benefits, their adoption is not without challenges.

Intermediate professionals may encounter difficulties in initially recognizing which pattern is most suitable for a given testing scenario or in integrating patterns into existing automation frameworks. Additionally, maintaining consistency across automated tests over time requires vigilance and periodic review to ensure patterns continue to align with evolving application requirements and industry best practices.

Moreover, the effectiveness of Test Automation Design Patterns depends heavily on the proficiency and collaboration of the QA team. Clear communication and knowledge sharing among team members are essential for ensuring that everyone understands and adheres to the established patterns consistently. Investing in training and skill development can empower intermediate professionals to leverage patterns effectively and contribute to the overall success of test automation initiatives within their organizations.

In conclusion, Test Automation Design Patterns represent a cornerstone of advanced test automation strategies for intermediate software QA engineers. By providing reusable solutions to common automation challenges, these patterns promote consistency, maintainability, and scalability within automated test suites. Their adoption facilitates efficient testing processes, enhances collaboration across teams, and ultimately contributes to delivering high-quality software products in a timely manner.

As software development continues to evolve, mastering Test Automation Design Patterns equips QA engineers with the tools needed to navigate complex automation scenarios effectively. Through continuous learning and practical application, intermediate professionals can leverage these patterns to elevate their automation skills and make meaningful contributions to their organizations' QA efforts.

Data-Driven Testing

In the dynamic realm of software development, where speed, accuracy, and reliability are critical, test automation plays a pivotal role in ensuring robust product quality. Among the methodologies available to software QA engineers, data-driven testing (DDT) has emerged as a powerful strategy to enhance the efficiency and effectiveness of automated testing processes.

Understanding Data-Driven Testing

Data-driven testing revolves around separating test scripts from test data. This approach allows QA teams to execute a single test script logic with multiple sets of input data, significantly increasing test coverage while maintaining manageable test scripts. By decoupling test logic from data inputs, DDT promotes reusability, scalability, and maintainability in test automation frameworks.

Fundamentally, DDT operates on the principle of variability. Instead of relying on predefined values within test scripts, testers leverage external data sources—such as spreadsheets, databases, or CSV files—to provide diverse input values to the same set of test scripts. This flexibility empowers QA teams to simulate a wide range of scenarios and edge cases, identifying potential bugs and vulnerabilities that might otherwise be overlooked.

Key Benefits of Data-Driven Testing

Implementing data-driven testing offers several tangible benefits that resonate throughout the software development lifecycle:

1. **Enhanced Test Coverage**: By systematically varying input values, DDT enables thorough validation of different user scenarios and system behaviors, thereby enhancing overall test coverage. This systematic approach reduces the risk of overlooking critical functionalities or edge cases that could impact product reliability.

2. **Improved Maintainability**: Separating test scripts from test data fosters modularity and ease of maintenance within automation frameworks. Updates or modifications to test scenarios can be swiftly implemented by adjusting the data sets, without requiring changes to the underlying test script logic. This modular design simplifies debugging processes and facilitates agile responses to evolving project requirements.

3. **Efficient Regression Testing**: In agile environments where frequent code changes occur, regression testing plays a crucial role in ensuring that new updates do not unintentionally introduce defects into previously functioning features. Data-driven testing automates the execution of regression test suites across multiple data sets, allowing QA teams to validate system stability and functionality efficiently.

4. **Optimized Resource Utilization**: DDT optimizes resource allocation by minimizing redundancy in test script development. Instead of creating separate scripts for each test scenario, QA engineers can reuse existing test logic across diverse data inputs. This streamlined approach reduces the effort required for test creation and execution, enabling teams to focus on strategic testing initiatives.

5. **Early Detection of Defects**: By systematically exploring various input combinations, data-driven testing facilitates early defect detection. QA engineers can uncover discrepancies in system behavior across different data permutations, enabling proactive resolution of potential issues before they escalate into more complex problems during later stages of development.

Implementation Best Practices

Successful implementation of data-driven testing depends on adhering to established best practices that promote efficiency, reliability, and scalability:

1. **Comprehensive Test Data Management**: Prioritize the creation and maintenance of high-quality test data sets that encompass a spectrum of realistic use cases and boundary conditions. Invest in robust data generation techniques to simulate diverse user inputs and system interactions effectively.

2. **Parameterization of Test Scripts**: Design test scripts with configurable parameters that facilitate dynamic data binding during test execution. Implement

frameworks or tools that support seamless integration between test logic and external data sources, ensuring flexibility and adaptability across different testing environments.

3. **Centralized Data Repositories**: Establish centralized repositories or libraries to store and manage test data artifacts securely. Utilize version control mechanisms to track changes and updates to test data sets, promoting consistency and traceability throughout the testing lifecycle.

4. **Cross-Functional Collaboration**: Foster collaboration between QA engineers, developers, and business stakeholders to align on data-driven testing strategies and priorities. Encourage interdisciplinary dialogue to leverage domain expertise and user insights in refining test scenarios and data sets.

5. **Continuous Evaluation and Optimization**: Implement a feedback-driven approach to continuously evaluate the effectiveness of data-driven testing initiatives. Monitor key metrics such as test coverage, defect density, and test execution time to identify areas for improvement and optimization within automation frameworks.

Challenges and Considerations

While data-driven testing offers compelling advantages, its adoption is not without challenges:

1. **Complex Test Data Dependencies**: Managing dependencies and relationships within large-scale data

sets can pose challenges in ensuring data integrity and consistency across test executions.

2. **Overhead in Test Data Maintenance**: The maintenance of extensive test data repositories requires diligent oversight and governance to mitigate the risk of data obsolescence or inaccuracies over time.

3. **Initial Setup and Configuration**: Configuring robust automation frameworks capable of seamlessly integrating with external data sources may require upfront investment in tool selection, configuration, and training.

4. **Performance Overhead**: Iteratively executing test scripts across multiple data sets can introduce performance overheads, necessitating optimization strategies to enhance test execution efficiency.

5. **Skill Set Requirements**: Effectively leveraging data-driven testing methodologies demands proficiency in scripting languages, data manipulation techniques, and automation tools, emphasizing the importance of continuous skill development and knowledge sharing within QA teams.

Future Directions

Looking ahead, the evolution of data-driven testing continues to be influenced by advancements in artificial intelligence, machine learning, and predictive analytics. Emerging technologies such as intelligent test data generation and autonomous test execution hold the potential to further streamline testing processes and enhance predictive test coverage.

In conclusion, data-driven testing represents a pivotal advancement in automated testing strategies available to software QA engineers. By harnessing the power of variability and scalability inherent in diverse data inputs, organizations can achieve heightened efficiency, improved test coverage, and accelerated time-to-market while upholding uncompromising standards of software quality and reliability. As the software development landscape evolves, embracing data-driven testing as a cornerstone of automated testing frameworks empowers QA teams to navigate complexities with agility and confidence, driving continuous innovation and excellence in software craftsmanship.

Keyword-Driven Testing

Among the various methodologies available to QA professionals, keyword-driven testing emerges as a sophisticated strategy tailored for the nuanced demands of modern software systems. This advanced approach transcends simple automation; it embodies a systematic framework that empowers teams to achieve comprehensive test coverage, streamline maintenance efforts, and enhance overall testing effectiveness.

Understanding Keyword-Driven Testing

Keyword-driven testing revolves around the principle of abstraction. It separates test design from test implementation, using a structured set of keywords that encapsulate specific actions, validations, or data manipulations. These keywords, similar to commands in a programming language, form the building blocks of test cases. They are carefully designed to align with functional requirements and user scenarios, offering a reusable and scalable framework adaptable to various testing needs.

Key Components and Workflow

The implementation of keyword-driven testing revolves around a few key components: keywords, test scripts, and a driver script or framework orchestrating their execution.

1. **Keywords**: These are fundamental units encapsulating specific test actions or validations. Examples include "login," "search," "verifyText," and "clickButton." Each keyword is defined with clear inputs, outputs, and expected behaviors, promoting clarity and reusability across different test cases.

2. **Test Scripts**: These scripts serve as the glue that integrates keywords into cohesive test scenarios. They outline the sequence of actions by calling relevant keywords in a structured manner, thereby simulating end-to-end user interactions.

3. **Driver Script/Framework**: Acting as the conductor of the testing process, the driver script or framework interprets high-level test instructions, selects appropriate test scripts, and executes them in a controlled environment. This layer of abstraction shields testers from low-level details, promoting modular design and facilitating easier maintenance.

Advantages of Keyword-Driven Testing

1. Modularity and Reusability:

Keywords encapsulate discrete functionalities, fostering modular test design. This modularity enhances reusability across multiple test cases and scenarios, minimizing redundancy and maintenance efforts. Teams can quickly create new test cases by rearranging existing keywords, promoting agility without compromising reliability.

2. Enhanced Test Coverage:

By mapping keywords to specific application functionalities, keyword-driven testing ensures comprehensive test coverage. Testers can construct detailed test scenarios that encompass diverse user interactions and edge cases, validating the robustness of the software under various conditions.

3. Reduced Maintenance Overhead:

The structured nature of keyword-driven testing mitigates maintenance challenges commonly associated with test automation. When application changes occur, updates are localized to relevant keywords or test scripts, sparing testers from the laborious task of rewriting entire test cases. This targeted approach not only saves time but also strengthens the sustainability of the test suite throughout the software's lifecycle.

4. Collaborative Framework:

Keyword-driven testing encourages collaboration between QA engineers and domain experts. By using a language of keywords that resonates with both technical and non-technical stakeholders, it promotes transparency and facilitates effective communication. This collaborative synergy ensures that test cases remain aligned with evolving business requirements and user expectations.

Implementing Keyword-Driven Testing

1. Initial Setup and Planning:

Successful implementation begins with meticulous planning. Identify key application functionalities and user scenarios to determine the necessary set of keywords. Collaborate with stakeholders to define clear expectations and acceptance criteria, establishing a robust foundation for subsequent testing phases.

2. Keyword Library Development:

Develop a comprehensive library of keywords tailored to the application's unique features and operations. Each keyword should encapsulate a specific action or validation, following a standardized naming convention and documentation. Establish guidelines for adding, modifying, or retiring keywords to maintain consistency and usability.

3. Test Case Authoring:

Craft test cases by assembling relevant keywords in a logical sequence. Define input parameters, expected outcomes, and any prerequisites necessary for test execution. Use data-driven techniques to validate various input combinations, ensuring thorough validation of application behavior across diverse scenarios.

4. Framework Development and Integration:

Build or leverage an existing test automation framework capable of orchestrating keyword-driven tests. Implement a modular architecture that supports dynamic loading of keywords, flexible test execution, and comprehensive reporting capabilities. Integrate the framework with continuous integration/continuous deployment (CI/CD) pipelines to automate test execution and seamlessly integrate it into the development lifecycle.

Challenges and Mitigation Strategies

1. Initial Learning Curve:

Transitioning to keyword-driven testing may present a learning curve for teams accustomed to traditional automation approaches. Provide comprehensive training sessions and practical workshops to familiarize testers with the methodology, emphasizing its benefits and practical application.

2. Keyword Maintenance:

Sustaining an evolving keyword library requires proactive maintenance strategies. Conduct regular reviews to evaluate keyword relevance and effectiveness in alignment with application updates. Implement version control mechanisms to track changes and facilitate rollback if necessary, preserving the integrity of the test suite.

3. Synchronization with Application Changes:

Maintain synchronization between application updates and corresponding test scripts. Utilize techniques such as version-specific keyword configurations or environment variables to accommodate dynamic changes without disrupting test continuity.

4. Tooling and Infrastructure:

Invest in robust automation tools and infrastructure capable of supporting keyword-driven testing requirements. Evaluate tools for compatibility with your chosen framework, scalability to accommodate growing test suites, and integration capabilities with existing QA environments.

Keyword-driven testing represents a pinnacle in test automation strategies, offering a structured framework that harmonizes precision with scalability. By abstracting test complexities into reusable keywords, teams can elevate their testing endeavors to new heights of efficiency and reliability. Embrace this methodology not merely as a tool for automation, but as a paradigm that empowers QA professionals to navigate the intricacies of modern software systems with confidence and efficacy. As technology advances, keyword-driven testing stands ready as a cornerstone of agile, quality-centric development practices, ensuring software systems meet the highest standards of functionality and performance.

Behavior-Driven Development (BDD)

Advanced test automation strategies like Behavior-Driven Development (BDD) have become essential methodologies for enhancing efficiency and reliability in software testing processes. BDD represents a significant shift from traditional testing methods by emphasizing collaboration among developers, testers, and domain experts. This collaborative approach ensures clear communication and alignment of goals throughout the software development lifecycle (SDLC).

Understanding Behavior-Driven Development (BDD)

Behavior-Driven Development builds on the principles of Test-Driven Development (TDD) but extends its focus beyond unit testing to encompass broader system behaviors. At its core, BDD emphasizes defining and validating software behavior from the perspective of stakeholders. This is facilitated through a shared language known as a ubiquitous language, which enables effective communication between technical and non-technical team members.

Key Components of BDD:

1. **Executable Specifications**: BDD promotes the creation of executable specifications using Gherkin, a structured format. Gherkin employs plain language syntax to describe how software should behave in various scenarios. These specifications serve as living documentation that guides development and verifies the correctness of implemented features.

2. **Collaborative Approach**: Unlike traditional methods that may isolate QA teams, BDD encourages collaboration among developers, testers, business analysts, and product owners. Involving all stakeholders in defining and refining feature requirements and acceptance criteria upfront helps prevent misunderstandings and ensures a shared understanding of desired outcomes.

3. **Integration of Automation**: BDD advocates for automating acceptance tests based on Gherkin scenarios defined during requirements gathering. Integrating automated testing into the development workflow enables early detection of defects and regressions, speeding up feedback and enhancing overall software quality.

Advantages of BDD in Test Automation

Implementing Behavior-Driven Development in test automation brings several significant advantages:

1. **Clarity and Alignment**: By using a ubiquitous language and structured scenarios, BDD promotes clear communication and alignment of development efforts with business objectives. This alignment reduces the risk of developing features that do not meet stakeholder expectations.

2. **Early Detection of Defects**: Automated acceptance tests developed through BDD scenarios enable teams to identify defects early in the SDLC. Early detection reduces the cost and effort required to fix issues discovered later in development.

3. **Improved Test Coverage**: BDD encourages comprehensive testing by focusing on critical business behaviors. This results in improved test coverage, ensuring that software meets functional requirements as defined by stakeholders.

4. **Enhanced Collaboration**: By involving stakeholders in creating and reviewing Gherkin scenarios, BDD

fosters collaboration where everyone contributes to validating software features. This collaborative effort results in higher-quality software that better meets user needs.

Implementing BDD: Best Practices and Considerations

Successful implementation of Behavior-Driven Development requires adhering to best practices and considering several factors:

1. **Securing Team Buy-In**: Success with BDD hinges on obtaining buy-in from all stakeholders, including developers, testers, and business representatives. Educating team members about BDD principles and demonstrating its impact on project outcomes is crucial.

2. **Effective Scenario Writing**: Writing effective Gherkin scenarios is essential for realizing the full benefits of BDD. Scenarios should be concise, unambiguous, and focused on describing specific behaviors in business-oriented language understandable to all stakeholders.

3. **Choosing the Right Automation Framework**: Selecting a suitable automation framework is critical for effective BDD implementation. Frameworks like Cucumber, SpecFlow, and Behat support executing Gherkin scenarios and integrate well with existing development tools and workflows.

4. **Continuous Refinement**: BDD emphasizes continuously refining Gherkin scenarios based on feedback and evolving project requirements. Regularly reviewing and updating scenarios ensures they remain aligned with business needs and reflect the latest software features.

Challenges and Mitigation Strategies

Despite its benefits, adopting Behavior-Driven Development may pose challenges that teams need to address proactively:

1. **Scenario Maintenance Overhead**: Managing numerous Gherkin scenarios can lead to maintenance overhead. To mitigate this challenge, teams should prioritize scenarios based on business impact and automate those offering the most value in terms of test coverage.

2. **Skill Set Requirements**: Effective BDD implementation requires team members proficient in both technical and domain-specific knowledge. Organizations may need to invest in training and skill development to ensure team members can write and automate Gherkin scenarios effectively.

3. **Cultural Resistance**: Introducing BDD may encounter resistance from teams accustomed to traditional testing methods. Overcoming cultural barriers involves emphasizing the collaborative benefits of BDD and supporting teams in transitioning smoothly to this methodology.

Behavior-Driven Development represents a significant advancement in test automation strategies, offering a structured approach to defining, automating, and validating software behaviors. By promoting collaboration, clear communication, and early defect detection, BDD enables teams to deliver higher-quality software aligned with stakeholder expectations. While implementing BDD requires addressing challenges and adopting best practices, the benefits of improved test coverage, enhanced collaboration, and accelerated feedback make it a valuable methodology for intermediate and advanced software QA professionals seeking to optimize their testing efforts in today's dynamic software development environment.

Chapter Three

Exploratory Testing

Understanding Exploratory Testing

Exploratory testing stands as a crucial technique in the toolkit of software QA engineers. Unlike scripted testing methods that follow predefined steps, exploratory testing embodies a flexible, adaptive approach driven by tester intuition, skill, and experience. This method is not just a departure from traditional testing routines but a dynamic strategy that thrives on the tester's ability to improvise, investigate, and uncover defects through active engagement with the software under examination.

At its heart, exploratory testing can be likened to an uncharted exploration where the tester navigates through the software application without predetermined routes or rigid plans. This methodological spontaneity allows testers to delve deeply into various aspects of the software, uncovering nuanced bugs and vulnerabilities that may evade scripted testing scenarios. The effectiveness of exploratory testing lies in its flexibility and its ability to simulate real-world usage conditions, providing a realistic assessment of the software's robustness.

One of the distinguishing features of exploratory testing is its reliance on the tester's cognitive abilities and domain knowledge. Unlike scripted tests that operate within predefined boundaries, exploratory testing encourages testers to leverage their understanding of the software's functionalities, user expectations, and potential edge cases. This proactive stance enables testers to simulate diverse user interactions, identify unexpected behaviors, and evaluate the software's response to unconventional inputs.

Moreover, exploratory testing promotes an iterative approach to quality assurance. Testers continuously refine their strategies based on immediate feedback from the software, adjusting their focus and priorities in real time. This iterative cycle not only enhances the efficiency of bug detection but also promotes a more comprehensive evaluation of the software's overall performance under varying conditions.

A critical aspect of exploratory testing lies in its adaptability to different stages of the software development lifecycle. Whether employed during initial feature development, regression testing, or post-release validation, this methodology offers unique advantages at each phase. Early-stage exploratory testing can uncover fundamental design flaws and usability issues, allowing teams to rectify them before they escalate into costly problems. Conversely, exploratory testing during regression phases helps ensure that new updates or fixes do not inadvertently introduce regressions into previously stable functionalities.

To execute exploratory testing effectively, testers must cultivate a multifaceted skill set that extends beyond technical proficiency. Communication skills play a pivotal role as testers collaborate closely with developers, product managers, and other stakeholders to convey findings, prioritize issues, and advocate for quality improvements. Furthermore, a keen analytical mindset coupled with an innate curiosity empowers testers to probe beneath the surface of the software, scrutinizing interactions and behaviors that automated scripts may overlook.

In practice, exploratory testing unfolds as an organic exploration of the software's features, functionalities, and user interfaces. Testers approach each testing session with an open mind, adapting their exploration paths based on evolving insights and observations. This flexibility enables testers to uncover intricate dependencies, assess error recovery mechanisms, and validate software resilience under unforeseen conditions.

Contrary to scripted testing methodologies that adhere to predefined test cases and expected outcomes, exploratory testing encourages testers to adopt a hands-on, investigatory approach. Testers actively manipulate inputs, observe system responses, and analyze outcomes in real time, thereby mimicking the unpredictable nature of user interactions. This empirical approach not only enhances the authenticity of test scenarios but also strengthens the software's overall resilience to unforeseen usage patterns.

The effectiveness of exploratory testing hinges on the tester's ability to strike a delicate balance between structured investigation and creative exploration. While the absence of predefined test cases may seem unconventional, this methodological fluidity empowers testers to uncover subtle defects, identify edge cases, and validate software assumptions that scripted tests may inadvertently overlook. Moreover, exploratory testing serves as a litmus test for the software's adaptability to evolving user expectations and operational environments.

Furthermore, exploratory testing offers a complementary perspective to automated testing frameworks by addressing scenarios that defy scripted prediction. Automated tests excel in repetitive tasks and regression checks but may struggle to simulate complex user interactions or assess software usability from a qualitative standpoint. In contrast, exploratory testing thrives on human intuition, adaptability, and real-time decision-making, making it an invaluable complement to automated testing strategies.

Beyond its tactical advantages, exploratory testing embodies a broader ethos of continuous improvement and quality assurance. By fostering a culture of exploration, inquiry, and collaboration within QA teams, organizations can cultivate a resilient testing mindset that transcends individual methodologies. This holistic approach not only enhances software quality but also instills a sense of ownership and accountability among testers, developers, and stakeholders alike.

Exploratory testing emerges not simply as a methodology but as a philosophy that champions adaptive exploration, empirical validation, and continuous improvement. By embracing the fluidity of exploratory testing, software QA engineers can transcend the limitations of scripted methodologies, uncover hidden defects, and fortify software resilience in an ever-changing technological landscape.

Exploratory Testing Techniques

Exploratory testing stands as a pivotal method in the toolkit of adept software quality assurance engineers. It represents a flexible approach to testing that avoids rigidly scripted test cases in favor of adaptive exploration of software functionality. Unlike traditional testing methods, exploratory testing is characterized by its spontaneity and emphasis on tester intuition and skill. This method not only complements structured testing but also serves as a crucial means for uncovering subtle defects and vulnerabilities that might evade detection.

The Essence of Exploratory Testing

Exploratory testing is fundamentally a cognitive activity where testers, drawing on their knowledge and experience, dynamically design and execute tests. This approach allows testers to adjust their strategies in real-time based on observed outcomes and evolving insights. By immersing themselves directly into the application, testers can simulate user interactions more authentically, thus replicating the natural usage patterns that end-users might adopt.

Techniques and Strategies in Exploratory Testing

1. Session-Based Testing:

- Central to effective exploratory testing is session-based testing. This structured approach divides exploratory testing into manageable sessions typically lasting from 60 to 120 minutes. During each session, testers concentrate on specific areas or aspects of the application, aiming to uncover defects efficiently while maintaining a record of activities performed and issues identified. This method ensures that testing efforts remain focused and productive, balancing exploration with accountability.

2. Heuristic Testing:

- Heuristic testing relies on heuristics, or rules of thumb, derived from the tester's experience and understanding of the application's behavior. Testers intuitively apply these heuristics to identify potential areas of weakness or instability within the software. Examples include boundary value analysis, where testers explore the edges of input ranges, or error guessing, where plausible error scenarios are hypothesized and tested. Heuristic testing encourages creative thinking and leverages the tester's analytical skills to unearth defects effectively.

3. Scenario-Based Testing:

- Scenario-based testing involves constructing realistic usage scenarios that mimic how end-users interact with the software. Testers devise these scenarios based on their understanding of user personas and typical workflows. By testing under these simulated conditions, testers can uncover usability issues, performance bottlenecks, and functional discrepancies that might impact user satisfaction. This approach ensures that the software not only meets functional requirements but also aligns with user expectations in diverse usage contexts.

4. Error-Oriented Testing:

- Error-oriented testing focuses on deliberately inducing errors or faults within the application to observe how the software responds. Testers intentionally inject faults such as invalid inputs, unexpected configurations, or environmental stressors to gauge the robustness and fault tolerance of the system. This method is particularly effective in validating error handling mechanisms and ensuring graceful degradation under adverse conditions. By proactively seeking out vulnerabilities, testers can preemptively address potential failure points before they manifest in production environments.

5. Exploratory Model-Based Testing:

- Exploratory model-based testing integrates exploratory techniques with formal modeling approaches, such as state transition diagrams or data flow diagrams. Testers use these models as guiding frameworks to explore different paths and states within the application dynamically. This hybrid approach combines the flexibility of exploratory testing with the structured analysis provided by formal models, enhancing test coverage and depth without sacrificing agility. It enables testers to navigate complex interactions and dependencies systematically, uncovering intricate defects that arise from nuanced system behaviors.

Advantages of Exploratory Testing

Exploratory testing offers several advantages that resonate deeply with the needs of modern software development and quality assurance:

- **Flexibility and Adaptability:** Unlike traditional testing methodologies that rely on predefined scripts, exploratory testing adapts seamlessly to changing requirements and evolving software functionalities.

Testers can adjust their focus and strategies in real-time, ensuring comprehensive test coverage in dynamic development environments.

- **Enhanced Test Coverage:** By encouraging testers to explore the application organically, exploratory testing facilitates broader test coverage across various user scenarios and edge cases. This comprehensive approach reduces the likelihood of undiscovered defects slipping into production, thereby enhancing overall software reliability and user satisfaction.

- **Early Defect Detection:** Through its proactive and intuitive nature, exploratory testing excels in identifying subtle defects and vulnerabilities early in the software development lifecycle. Testers leverage their domain expertise to pinpoint potential issues swiftly, allowing developers to address them promptly and cost-effectively.

- **User-Centric Validation:** By simulating real-world usage scenarios and user interactions, exploratory testing validates the software from a user-centric perspective. This validation ensures that the application not only meets functional requirements but also delivers an intuitive and seamless user experience, thereby fostering user adoption and loyalty.

Challenges and Considerations

While exploratory testing offers significant advantages, it is not without challenges and considerations:

- **Documentation and Traceability:** Unlike scripted testing, exploratory testing may lack explicit documentation of test cases and steps followed. Ensuring adequate documentation and traceability of testing activities is essential for maintaining accountability and facilitating collaboration across development teams.

- **Skill and Expertise:** Effective exploratory testing relies heavily on the tester's experience, intuition, and domain knowledge. Organizations must invest in continuous training and skill development to cultivate proficient exploratory testers capable of maximizing the technique's benefits.

- **Coverage and Reproducibility:** The organic nature of exploratory testing can sometimes lead to variations in test coverage and reproducibility of results. Establishing clear testing objectives and guidelines, while allowing for flexibility, helps mitigate these challenges and ensures consistent quality assurance practices.

Exploratory testing represents a dynamic and indispensable technique within the toolkit of software quality assurance professionals. By empowering testers to explore software functionality intuitively and adaptively, exploratory testing enhances test coverage, accelerates defect detection, and fosters user-centric validation. Leveraging techniques such as session-based testing, heuristic testing, and scenario-based testing, testers can uncover nuanced defects that traditional testing methodologies might overlook. While challenges such as documentation and skill development require attention, the benefits of exploratory testing in improving software quality and user satisfaction are unmistakable. As software development continues to evolve, exploratory testing remains a pivotal approach in ensuring the delivery of robust, reliable, and user-friendly applications.

Tools for Exploratory Testing

Exploratory testing is a fundamental practice in modern software quality assurance. It offers a flexible and adaptive approach to uncovering defects and evaluating system behavior, distinct from scripted testing methods. Instead of following predefined paths and expected outcomes, exploratory testing empowers testers to actively engage with the software, using their expertise and intuition to explore its nuances and potential vulnerabilities.

The Essence of Exploratory Testing

At its core, exploratory testing is characterized by its responsiveness and adaptability. Testers are not constrained by rigid test scripts but can dynamically create and execute test cases based on real-time observations and insights gained during testing sessions. This approach allows testers to discover issues that might be overlooked in scripted testing scenarios, responding effectively to unexpected behaviors and anomalies as they arise.

Key Principles and Benefits

Flexibility and Creativity

One of the fundamental principles of exploratory testing is its flexibility. Testers have the freedom to adjust their testing approach based on initial findings, emerging risks, or changing project needs. This flexibility fosters creativity, enabling testers to explore diverse scenarios and edge cases that may not have been considered during initial test planning.

Rapid Feedback and Issue Identification

Exploratory testing excels in providing rapid feedback to development teams. By actively exploring the software and interacting with it in real-time, testers can quickly identify and report critical issues and usability concerns. This immediacy is particularly valuable in agile environments where quick feedback loops are essential.

Enhanced Tester Engagement and Responsibility

Unlike scripted testing, which can sometimes be mechanical, exploratory testing encourages active engagement and responsibility among testers. Testers immerse themselves in the application, utilizing their skills and experience to uncover defects and assess overall system quality. This hands-on approach not only enhances the thoroughness of testing but also boosts tester motivation and satisfaction.

Tools and Techniques for Exploratory Testing

While exploratory testing relies heavily on human judgment and experience, several tools and techniques can enhance its effectiveness:

Session-Based Test Management (SBTM)

SBTM provides a structured framework for conducting exploratory testing sessions. Testers define session objectives and prioritize areas of focus, documenting their findings in real-time. Tools such as Microsoft Test Manager and Session Tester facilitate session management, helping testers maintain focus and track progress during exploratory testing activities.

Mind Mapping Tools

Mind mapping tools like MindMeister or XMind are invaluable for organizing test ideas and visualizing test coverage during exploratory testing. Testers can use these tools to brainstorm test scenarios, connect related concepts, and explore different pathways through the software. This visual representation aids in maintaining comprehensive test coverage and identifying potential gaps in testing efforts.

Screen Recording and Annotation Tools

Screen recording tools such as Camtasia or OBS Studio allow testers to capture their interactions with the software interface during exploratory testing sessions. These recordings serve as detailed documentation of test activities, enabling testers to revisit specific scenarios, reproduce issues, and share findings with stakeholders. Annotation features within these tools further enhance communication by highlighting key observations and explaining testing decisions.

Bug Tracking and Collaboration Platforms

Effective communication and collaboration are essential for successful exploratory testing. Bug tracking systems like Jira or Bugzilla facilitate the capture, prioritization, and resolution of defects identified during testing. Integration with collaboration platforms such as Slack or Microsoft Teams enables real-time communication between testers, developers, and other project stakeholders, promoting a collaborative approach to defect management.

Automated Exploratory Testing Tools

While human judgment is paramount in exploratory testing, automated tools can complement testing efforts by performing repetitive tasks and providing additional insights. Tools like Tricentis Tosca or Selenium IDE offer capabilities for recording test actions, generating test scripts, and executing exploratory test scenarios in a controlled manner. These tools streamline exploratory testing activities, allowing testers to focus on critical analysis and exploration.

Best Practices for Effective Exploratory Testing

To maximize the benefits of exploratory testing, consider the following best practices:

Define Clear Objectives and Session Goals

Before conducting an exploratory testing session, establish clear objectives and session goals. Define the scope of testing, prioritize areas of interest, and communicate expectations with stakeholders. Clear objectives guide testers in their exploratory efforts and ensure alignment with project objectives.

Encourage Collaboration and Knowledge Sharing

Promote collaboration between testers, developers, and other stakeholders throughout the exploratory testing process. Share insights, discuss test findings, and collaborate on identifying potential improvements. Cross-functional collaboration enhances understanding of system behavior and fosters shared responsibility for software quality.

Embrace Iterative Testing and Continuous Improvement

Exploratory testing is iterative and adaptive by nature. Embrace a cycle of continuous learning and improvement by incorporating feedback from previous testing sessions, refining testing strategies, and exploring new test scenarios. Adopting a growth mindset encourages innovation and flexibility in responding to evolving project requirements.

Document Findings and Maintain Comprehensive Coverage

Systematically document test findings, observations, and identified issues during exploratory testing sessions. Maintain comprehensive test coverage by revisiting session goals, updating test documentation, and ensuring traceability of test activities. Effective documentation supports knowledge transfer, informs future testing efforts, and facilitates informed decision-making.

Exploratory testing is a dynamic and essential approach to software quality assurance, combining structured testing practices with the freedom to explore and innovate. By leveraging human intuition, creativity, and adaptability, testers can uncover critical defects, evaluate system behavior, and enhance overall software quality. Complemented by various tools and techniques, exploratory testing empowers testers to navigate complexities, respond to emerging risks, and contribute to the success of software projects. As organizations increasingly adopt agile methodologies and prioritize continuous delivery, the role of exploratory testing in ensuring robust software solutions remains pivotal. By embracing the principles and best practices outlined, software QA professionals can harness the full potential of exploratory testing to deliver reliable, user-centric software products in today's competitive environment,

Integrating Exploratory Testing with Formal Testing

Exploratory testing represents a dynamic approach to software quality assurance that complements structured methodologies by embracing adaptability and creativity in testing processes. Unlike formal testing, which follows predefined scripts and test cases, exploratory testing relies on the tester's intuition, experience, and analytical skills to uncover defects and assess software behavior in real-time. This method not only enhances test coverage but also provides valuable insights into the user experience and potential edge cases that scripted testing might overlook.

Understanding Exploratory Testing

At its core, exploratory testing is about exploration and discovery within the software under test (SUT). It involves simultaneous learning, test design, and execution, driven by the tester's understanding of the application and its intended functionality. This approach allows testers to adapt their strategies based on early feedback, making it particularly effective in agile environments where continuous integration and rapid deployment are common practices.

The Role of Creativity and Intuition

Unlike formal testing, which can be repetitive and rigid, exploratory testing encourages testers to think outside the box. Testers leverage their domain knowledge and expertise to simulate real-world scenarios, uncovering defects that scripted tests might not catch. This creative aspect of exploratory testing fosters innovation in defect detection and helps refine test cases based on observed behaviors and patterns.

Benefits of Exploratory Testing

1. **Early Bug Detection**: By exploring the software dynamically, testers can identify critical defects early in the development lifecycle, reducing costs associated with late-stage bug fixes.

2. **Enhanced Test Coverage**: Exploratory testing complements formal testing by covering areas that scripted tests might miss, thereby providing more comprehensive test coverage.

3. **Real-Time Feedback**: Testers can provide immediate feedback to developers, facilitating quicker resolutions and enhancing collaboration between teams.

4. **User-Centric Approach**: Since exploratory testing mimics user interactions, it helps ensure that the software meets end-user expectations and addresses usability issues effectively.

Integrating Exploratory Testing with Formal Testing

While exploratory testing offers numerous advantages, it is most effective when integrated with formal testing methodologies rather than viewed as a standalone approach. This integration creates a balanced testing strategy that leverages the strengths of both methods, optimizing test coverage and defect detection throughout the software development lifecycle.

Structured Test Planning

Formal testing frameworks, such as test plans and automated test suites, provide structure and repeatability essential for regression testing and baseline validation. These formal processes ensure that core functionalities and critical paths are thoroughly tested, meeting predefined quality standards and compliance requirements.

Agile Adaptability

In agile environments, where requirements evolve rapidly, exploratory testing shines by accommodating changes and facilitating quick feedback loops. Testers can adjust their exploration based on evolving user stories and acceptance criteria, ensuring that new features and enhancements are thoroughly validated before release.

Synergistic Test Execution

Integrating exploratory testing sessions into sprint cycles or release milestones allows for synergy between exploratory and formal testing efforts. Testers can execute scripted tests to validate expected behaviors while concurrently exploring uncharted areas and edge cases through ad-hoc testing. This dual approach maximizes defect detection and mitigates risks associated with software complexity.

Continuous Improvement

Central to integrating exploratory testing with formal testing is the emphasis on continuous improvement. Testers document their exploratory sessions, including identified defects and test scenarios, which informs future test design and refines formal test cases. This iterative process fosters a learning culture within QA teams, enhancing overall test effectiveness and efficiency over time.

Practical Considerations and Best Practices

Training and Skill Development

Effective exploratory testing requires honed skills in critical thinking, risk assessment, and software analysis. Investing in continuous training programs and workshops equips testers with the necessary competencies to conduct insightful exploratory sessions and maximize test coverage.

Test Environment Management

Maintaining diverse test environments that mirror production configurations is essential for realistic exploratory testing. Testers need access to varied platforms, devices, and network conditions to simulate diverse user scenarios and uncover platform-specific issues effectively.

Collaboration and Communication

Successful integration of exploratory testing hinges on strong collaboration between QA, development, and product teams.

Clear communication of test findings, including identified defects and usability concerns, fosters transparency and expedites issue resolution across teams.

Metrics and Reporting

Establishing meaningful metrics for exploratory testing, such as defect density and test coverage gaps, provides stakeholders with quantifiable insights into test effectiveness. Regular reporting on exploratory findings alongside formal test results ensures comprehensive visibility into software quality status and informs decision-making processes.

Exploratory testing enriches traditional QA practices by infusing adaptability, creativity, and real-time feedback into the testing process. When integrated thoughtfully with formal testing methodologies, it enhances test coverage, accelerates defect detection, and promotes a user-centric approach to software quality assurance. By embracing exploratory testing as a complementary strategy, organizations can foster innovation, improve product quality, and deliver software that meets evolving user expectations in today's dynamic digital environments.

Chapter Four

Test Management and Leadership

Test Management Principles

Test management in software quality assurance (QA) involves strategically coordinating activities to ensure the delivery of high-quality software products. It serves as a pivotal framework encompassing planning, monitoring, and controlling the testing process throughout the software development lifecycle (SDLC). Effective test management requires a blend of technical proficiency, leadership prowess, and a deep understanding of organizational dynamics.

The Role of Test Management

At its core, test management integrates closely with project management to align testing efforts with overall development goals. This integration ensures proactive rather than reactive testing, anticipating challenges early in the development cycle to prevent defects from impacting subsequent phases. This proactive stance reduces rework and ensures cost-effective delivery of quality software.

Principles of Effective Test Management

1. Strategic Planning:

Effective test management begins with meticulous planning that defines the scope, objectives, and timelines of testing activities. Collaborating closely with stakeholders aligns testing strategies with business objectives. Strategic planning also involves allocating resources appropriately to ensure that the necessary personnel, tools, and environments are available for effective testing.

2. Comprehensive Test Strategy:

A robust test strategy forms the foundation of effective test management. It encompasses various testing types - from functional and non-functional testing to regression and performance testing - tailored to the specific needs of the software under development. It involves selecting appropriate testing techniques, designing test cases, and establishing metrics to measure progress and effectiveness.

3. Risk Management:

Mitigating risks is integral to effective test management. Identifying potential risks early in the SDLC allows test managers to prioritize testing efforts and allocate resources accordingly. Risk-based testing ensures critical functionalities and vulnerable areas of the software receive thorough testing, minimizing the likelihood of defects reaching production..

4. Quality Assurance Metrics

Test management relies on metrics to assess the quality and progress of testing activities. Metrics such as defect density, test coverage, and test execution metrics provide quantitative insights into the effectiveness of testing efforts. These metrics support informed decision-making and serve as indicators of the software's readiness for release.

5. Effective Communication:

Clear and concise communication is essential in test management. Test managers act as intermediaries between QA teams, development teams, and project stakeholders, ensuring transparency and alignment of expectations. Effective communication fosters collaboration, facilitates issue resolution, and promotes a shared commitment to delivering a high-quality product.

6. Continuous Improvement:

Test management thrives on continuous improvement. Post-mortem analysis, retrospectives, and lessons learned sessions provide opportunities to refine testing processes and practices. Adopting agile methodologies supports iterative improvement, allowing test managers to adapt quickly to evolving requirements and technological advancements.

Leadership in Test Management

Leadership in test management extends beyond traditional management roles, encompassing vision, inspiration, and the ability to influence stakeholders towards achieving quality goals. Effective test leaders demonstrate several key attributes:

1. Visionary Thinking:

Test leaders envision quality as fundamental to software development, inspiring teams to pursue excellence in testing. They articulate a compelling vision that aligns testing efforts with organizational objectives, cultivating a culture of quality throughout the SDLC.

2 . Empowering Teams:

Empowerment is central to effective leadership. Test managers empower their teams by fostering collaboration, encouraging innovation, and facilitating skill development. Empowered teams demonstrate greater ownership and accountability, driving productivity and creativity in testing endeavors.

3. Decision-Making Acumen::

Test leaders possess the ability to make informed decisions amidst uncertainty. They leverage data-driven insights, stakeholder input, and their own expertise to navigate complex testing challenges and prioritize efforts effectively. Decisive leadership ensures that testing activities remain on track, even amidst evolving project dynamics.

4. Change Management:

Adaptability is crucial in a dynamic software development environment. Test leaders adeptly manage change by anticipating potential disruptions, aligning testing strategies with evolving requirements, and championing agile practices. They foster resilience and flexibility, enabling teams to respond promptly to shifting priorities and market demands.

5. Ethical Leadership:

Ethical considerations underpin leadership in test management. Test leaders uphold integrity, transparency, and fairness in their interactions with teams, stakeholders, and customers. They advocate for ethical testing practices, ensuring that quality is never compromised for expediency or competitive advantage.

Challenges and Future Directions

Despite its pivotal role, test management faces challenges in a complex digital environment. Rapid technological advancements, shorter development cycles, and the widespread adoption of agile and DevOps methodologies require ongoing adaptation and innovation in test management practices. Future directions include:

- **Automation and AI:** Utilizing automation and artificial intelligence to enhance testing efficiency, accuracy, and coverage.
- **Shift-Left Testing:** Embedding testing early in the SDLC to identify and mitigate defects at the source.
- **Continuous Testing:** Integrating testing seamlessly into CI/CD pipelines to ensure rapid feedback and continuous quality assurance.
- **Metrics-driven Quality:** Evolving towards more sophisticated metrics and analytics to measure and enhance the effectiveness of testing efforts.

Test management is pivotal in software quality assurance, integrating strategic planning, effective leadership, and continuous improvement to deliver high-quality software products. By embracing proactive strategies, fostering collaboration, and advocating for ethical practices, test managers and leaders can navigate challenges, inspire innovation, and uphold the promise of quality in today's dynamic digital environment. As technology evolves, so too must test management evolve, adapting to meet the demands of modern software development challenges.

Test Estimation Techniques

Effective test management and leadership are crucial for ensuring the delivery of reliable and high-quality products. One of the critical aspects of this discipline is test estimation, a process that demands precision, foresight, and a deep understanding of both technical and managerial aspects.

Understanding Test Estimation

Test estimation is the systematic process of predicting the effort, time, and resources required for testing activities within a software development project. It serves as a crucial element in project planning, influencing decisions on budgeting, resource allocation, and timelines. The accuracy of test estimation directly impacts project success, influencing stakeholders' confidence in the QA process and the overall delivery schedule.

Importance of Accurate Test Estimation

Accurate estimation is paramount for several reasons. Firstly, it facilitates realistic project planning, allowing teams to set achievable goals and allocate resources efficiently. Secondly, it aids in managing stakeholders' expectations by providing transparent insights into the testing process's scope and duration. Thirdly, it enables proactive risk management, identifying potential challenges early in the project lifecycle.

Challenges in Test Estimation

Despite its significance, test estimation poses several challenges. One primary challenge is the inherent uncertainty in software development, where requirements may evolve, scope may change, or unexpected issues may arise. Additionally, the complexity of modern software systems and the interconnectedness of components make it difficult to predict testing efforts accurately. Moreover, estimating testing efforts for new technologies or domains adds another layer of complexity, requiring expertise and research.

Techniques for Test Estimation

Several established techniques help QA professionals navigate these challenges and achieve reliable test estimations:

1. Expert Judgment

Expert judgment leverages the insights and experience of seasoned QA professionals, project managers, and domain experts. By pooling collective knowledge, teams can identify potential risks, dependencies, and nuances that impact testing efforts. This technique is valuable in early project stages when detailed data may be scarce, relying instead on qualitative assessments and historical data from similar projects.

2. Historical Data Analysis

Analyzing historical data from past projects provides empirical insights into testing efforts based on similar contexts, technologies, and team dynamics. This data-driven approach enhances the accuracy of estimations by identifying trends, patterns, and recurring challenges. It enables teams to make informed decisions and adjustments based on real-world metrics rather than hypothetical scenarios.

3. Parametric Estimation

Parametric estimation employs mathematical models and algorithms to calculate testing efforts based on measurable project parameters such as lines of code, function points, or test case counts. These models derive estimates by correlating historical data with project-specific variables, offering a quantitative basis for predictions. Parametric estimation is particularly effective in large-scale projects with well-defined metrics and established benchmarks.

4. Three-Point Estimation (PERT)

The PERT technique combines optimistic, pessimistic, and most likely scenarios to derive a weighted average estimate. By considering best-case, worst-case, and expected outcomes, QA teams can account for uncertainties and variability in project requirements. PERT fosters a probabilistic approach to test estimation, providing a range of possible outcomes and the likelihood of achieving them.

5. Delphi Technique

The Delphi technique engages a panel of experts in iterative rounds of estimation and consensus-building. Participants anonymously contribute their estimates, review collective feedback, and revise their assessments until a convergence of opinions is reached. This method fosters collaboration, minimizes biases, and accommodates diverse perspectives, leading to more robust and reliable estimations.

Best Practices in Test Estimation

To enhance the effectiveness of test estimation, QA leaders and managers should adopt the following best practices:

- **Collaborative Approach:** Involve stakeholders, developers, and QA teams early in the estimation process to foster shared understanding and commitment.
- **Iterative Refinement:** Continuously refine estimations as new information becomes available, ensuring alignment with evolving project dynamics.
- **Risk-Based Estimation:** Prioritize testing efforts based on criticality and potential impact, focusing resources where they are most needed.
- **Documentation and Tracking:** Maintain clear documentation of estimation assumptions, methodologies, and rationale to facilitate transparency and accountability.
- **Post-Implementation Review:** Conduct post-mortem reviews to evaluate the accuracy of initial estimations, identify lessons learned, and improve future estimation practices.

Effective test estimation is indispensable for successful software QA management and leadership. By employing a combination of expert judgment, historical data analysis, parametric models, PERT, and the Delphi technique, QA professionals can navigate the complexities of software testing with confidence and precision. Embracing best practices such as collaboration, iterative refinement, risk-based prioritization, and continuous improvement ensures that test estimations not only meet project requirements but also contribute to overall project success. Mastering test estimation remains a cornerstone of excellence in QA engineering, guiding teams towards delivering robust, reliable, and high-quality software products.

Test Team Leadership

The role of a Test Team Leader stands as a crucial cornerstone in ensuring the effectiveness and success of software testing efforts. This advanced handbook delves into the complex responsibilities and refined skills that define effective leadership within a QA testing environment.

Understanding the Role of a Test Team Leader

At its core, the role of a Test Team Leader encompasses far more than overseeing testing activities. It necessitates a deep understanding of both technical aspects and human dynamics. A proficient leader in this capacity not only orchestrates the testing processes but also fosters a cohesive and high-performing team.

Technical Proficiency and Strategic Oversight

Technical expertise forms the foundation upon which effective leadership in software QA is built. A Test Team Leader must possess a comprehensive grasp of testing methodologies, automation frameworks, and industry-specific tools. This proficiency enables informed decision-making and strategic planning, crucial for guiding the team through complex testing scenarios.

Beyond technical prowess, strategic oversight plays a pivotal role. It involves aligning testing activities with overarching project goals and timelines, thereby ensuring that QA efforts contribute meaningfully to the project's success. This strategic alignment demands foresight and the ability to anticipate potential bottlenecks or challenges in the testing process.

Cultivating a High-Performance Team

A hallmark of exceptional leadership lies in the leader's ability to nurture a high-performance team culture. This entails fostering an environment where team members are motivated, empowered, and equipped to excel in their roles. Effective communication, mentorship, and recognition of individual contributions are integral to fostering team cohesion and morale.

Furthermore, a Test Team Leader must adeptly manage team dynamics and interpersonal relationships. This includes resolving conflicts, leveraging team strengths, and fostering a collaborative spirit among diverse team members. By promoting open dialogue and constructive feedback, leaders can harness the collective expertise of the team towards achieving testing objectives with efficiency and precision.

Key Responsibilities and Strategic Initiatives

Defining Test Strategies and Processes

Central to the role of a Test Team Leader is the formulation of comprehensive test strategies and processes. This involves collaborating closely with stakeholders to understand project requirements, risks, and quality goals. By delineating clear testing objectives and methodologies, leaders provide a roadmap for the team's activities, ensuring that testing efforts are systematic and methodical.

Resource Allocation and Optimization

Effective resource management is another critical aspect of leadership in software QA. Test Team Leaders must allocate resources judiciously, balancing workload distribution with team members' skills and capabilities. This involves identifying areas where automation can streamline repetitive tasks, thereby optimizing efficiency without compromising on test coverage or quality.

Moreover, proactive resource planning enables leaders to anticipate resource constraints or dependencies early in the project lifecycle. By advocating for adequate resources and advocating for necessary tools or infrastructure, leaders empower their teams to execute testing initiatives effectively and mitigate potential risks proactively.

Stakeholder Communication and Relationship Management

Communication lies at the heart of effective leadership in QA testing. Test Team Leaders serve as the primary liaison between the QA team and other project stakeholders, including developers, product managers, and senior leadership. Clear and concise communication of testing progress, issues, and insights is essential for fostering transparency and alignment across the project.

Furthermore, cultivating strong relationships with stakeholders engenders trust and credibility in the QA process. By soliciting feedback, addressing concerns promptly, and advocating for QA priorities, leaders demonstrate their commitment to delivering high-quality software products that meet or exceed stakeholder expectations.

Challenges and Strategies for Success

Managing Complexity and Change

The dynamic nature of software development presents inherent challenges for Test Team Leaders. Rapid iterations, evolving requirements, and shifting priorities necessitate adaptability and resilience in leadership. Leaders must navigate ambiguity and complexity with agility, adjusting test strategies and priorities as project dynamics evolve.

Strategies for managing complexity include establishing robust change management processes and fostering a culture of continuous improvement within the QA team. By embracing iterative testing practices and leveraging feedback loops, leaders can iteratively refine testing approaches and adapt to changing project landscapes without compromising on quality or delivery timelines.

Promoting Innovation and Continuous Learning

Innovation is a cornerstone of effective QA leadership. Test Team Leaders should encourage experimentation with new tools, technologies, and methodologies that enhance testing efficiency and effectiveness. By fostering a culture of innovation, leaders empower their teams to explore novel approaches to testing and adopt industry best practices that drive continuous improvement.

Additionally, promoting continuous learning is essential for staying abreast of emerging trends and evolving industry standards. Leaders should invest in professional development opportunities for team members, such as training workshops, certifications, or participation in industry conferences. By cultivating a learning mindset within the team, leaders foster a culture of expertise and innovation that propels QA initiatives forward.

The role of a Test Team Leader in software QA is multifaceted and pivotal to the success of testing endeavors. Beyond technical proficiency, effective leadership entails strategic oversight, team cultivation, and adept management of stakeholder relationships. By championing clear communication, proactive resource management, and a commitment to innovation and continuous learning, leaders can navigate challenges and propel their teams towards achieving excellence in software quality assurance. As software development continues to evolve, the role of Test Team Leaders remains indispensable in ensuring the delivery of high-quality, reliable software products that meet the needs and expectations of stakeholders and end-users alike.

Managing Test Environments

Effective test management and leadership are essential for ensuring the reliability and functionality of software systems. Among the numerous responsibilities of a QA engineer, managing test environments stands out as a critical aspect that demands meticulous planning, strategic thinking, and adept execution.

Understanding Test Environments

Before diving into the intricacies of managing test environments, it's crucial to grasp what constitutes a test environment in software testing. A test environment replicates the production environment to a significant extent, allowing QA engineers to conduct comprehensive testing of software applications before deploying them for actual use. This setup includes hardware, software, network configurations, and other dependencies that closely mimic the conditions where the software will operate.

The Role of Test Environment Management

Effective management of test environments involves overseeing the entire lifecycle of these setups, from their initial creation to their eventual retirement. This encompasses a series of interconnected tasks and decisions aimed at ensuring that the test environment remains stable, accurate, and conducive to rigorous testing activities throughout the software development lifecycle (SDLC).

Key Challenges in Test Environment Management

Managing test environments poses several challenges that require proactive management and strategic solutions. One primary challenge is synchronizing test environments with ongoing development efforts. As software progresses through various stages of development, the test environment must keep pace to accurately reflect these changes. Failure to synchronize can lead to discrepancies between test results and actual system behavior in production, undermining the entire testing process.

Another significant challenge is allocating resources for test environments. Depending on the scale and complexity of the software project, multiple test environments may be necessary, each with specific configurations and resources tailored to different testing scenarios. Securing adequate resources, including hardware, software licenses, and testing tools, becomes crucial to maintaining the integrity and effectiveness of the testing process.

Best Practices in Test Environment Management

To navigate these challenges effectively, QA teams employ several best practices in managing test environments:

1. **Standardization and Automation:** Standardizing the configuration of test environments and automating their setup and teardown processes can streamline management efforts and reduce the risk of human error. Automation tools and scripts play a pivotal role in achieving consistency and repeatability across different testing environments.

2. **Configuration Management:** Implementing robust configuration management practices ensures that changes to the test environment are controlled and documented. Version control systems and configuration management tools help track changes, manage dependencies, and facilitate collaboration among team members working on different aspects of the test environment.

3. **Monitoring and Maintenance:** Continuous monitoring of test environments is essential to detect issues such as performance bottlenecks, resource constraints, or configuration drifts. Proactive maintenance, including regular updates and patches, helps keep test environments stable and aligned with evolving project requirements.

4. **Collaboration and Communication:** Effective communication and collaboration between QA engineers, developers, and other stakeholders are crucial for aligning the goals of test environment management with overall project objectives. Clear communication ensures that everyone involved understands the status of test environments, upcoming changes, and any potential impacts on testing activities.

5. **Capacity Planning:** Anticipating future testing needs and planning for scalability in test environments are vital aspects of effective management. Capacity planning involves assessing current and future resource requirements based on project timelines, expected workload, and potential growth in the user base.

Leadership in Test Environment Management

Beyond technical proficiency, leadership in test environment management requires a blend of strategic vision, communication skills, and the ability to align testing efforts with broader business goals. Test environment managers play a pivotal role in:

- **Setting Clear Objectives:** Establishing clear objectives for test environment management that align with project milestones and quality metrics ensures that testing efforts contribute meaningfully to the overall success of the software project.

- **Risk Management:** Identifying and mitigating risks associated with test environments, such as data security vulnerabilities or compatibility issues, helps safeguard the integrity and confidentiality of testing processes.

- **Continuous Improvement:** Encouraging a culture of continuous improvement where feedback from testing activities is used to refine and enhance test environments over time. This includes adopting new technologies, methodologies, or tools that can optimize testing efficiency and effectiveness.
- **Stakeholder Engagement:** Engaging with stakeholders across different departments, including development teams, project managers, and business analysts, to solicit input, address concerns, and foster collaboration in achieving shared objectives related to test environment management.

Effective test environment management is essential for ensuring the quality, reliability, and functionality of software applications. By implementing best practices, leveraging automation tools, and fostering strong leadership, QA engineers can navigate the complexities of managing test environments with confidence and efficiency. Ultimately, a well-managed test environment not only facilitates thorough testing but also contributes to the overall success of software projects by identifying and addressing potential issues early in the development lifecycle.

Chapter Five

Risk-Based Testing

Introduction to Risk-Based Testing

Ensuring the quality of deliverables is paramount. Among the various methodologies and approaches that aim to enhance the effectiveness of testing, Risk-Based Testing (RBT) stands out as a strategic approach that aligns testing activities with project risks. This methodological framework acknowledges that not all tests are created equal; rather, their prioritization should be guided by the potential impact of failures on the project's objectives.

Understanding Risk-Based Testing

At its core, Risk-Based Testing revolves around the identification, assessment, and prioritization of risks inherent in the software under test. This approach acknowledges that software systems are susceptible to various risks, ranging from technical complexities to user requirements volatility and environmental dependencies. By assessing these risks early in the project lifecycle, teams can strategically allocate testing efforts where they are most needed.

Key Principles of Risk-Based Testing

1. Risk Assessment

The foundation of Risk-Based Testing lies in comprehensive risk assessment. This involves identifying potential risks that could impact the software's functionality, performance, security, or usability. Risks are not only limited to technical aspects but also encompass business and operational considerations. Through workshops, brainstorming sessions, and leveraging past project data, teams identify and categorize risks based on their likelihood and potential impact.

2. Risk Prioritization

Once risks are identified, the next critical step is prioritization. Risks are prioritized based on their severity and the consequences of their occurrence. Risks that pose a high probability of occurrence and have severe consequences are prioritized higher than those with lower impact. This prioritization guides the allocation of resources and determines the depth and breadth of testing activities.

3. Tailored Testing Strategies

Unlike traditional testing approaches that follow a predefined set of test cases, Risk-Based Testing advocates for tailored testing strategies. Tests are designed to address the identified risks effectively. This means focusing on critical functionalities, boundary conditions, and scenarios that have the highest risk exposure. By aligning testing efforts with identified risks, teams can optimize testing coverage while maximizing risk mitigation.

4. Continuous Risk Monitoring

Risk management in software projects is not a one-time activity but a continuous process. Throughout the project lifecycle, risks evolve due to changes in requirements, technology, or market conditions. Risk-Based Testing emphasizes continuous risk monitoring and adaptation of testing strategies accordingly. Regular reviews and updates ensure that testing efforts remain aligned with the current project risks and objectives.

Benefits of Risk-Based Testing

1. Enhanced Risk Coverage

By focusing testing efforts on high-risk areas, Risk-Based Testing improves risk coverage. This targeted approach ensures that critical functionalities and potential failure points are thoroughly tested, reducing the likelihood of major defects slipping into production.

2. Efficient Resource Allocation

Traditional testing approaches often allocate resources uniformly across all test scenarios, regardless of their criticality. In contrast, Risk-Based Testing optimizes resource allocation by directing efforts where they are most needed. This leads to a more efficient use of time, budget, and manpower throughout the testing phase.

3. Early Defect Detection

Prioritizing testing based on risks increases the likelihood of detecting critical defects early in the development cycle. Early defect detection minimizes rework efforts and associated costs, as issues are identified and addressed proactively before they escalate into larger problems.

4. Improved Stakeholder Confidence

Effective risk management through Risk-Based Testing enhances stakeholder confidence in the software's quality and reliability. By demonstrating a systematic approach to risk mitigation and testing, teams can instill trust among stakeholders, including clients, end-users, and project sponsors.

Implementing Risk-Based Testing

1. Establishing a Risk Management Framework

Successful implementation of Risk-Based Testing begins with establishing a robust risk management framework. This framework defines processes and guidelines for identifying, assessing, and prioritizing risks across the project lifecycle. It also outlines roles and responsibilities, ensuring that risk management activities are integrated seamlessly into the overall project management process.

2. Collaboration and Communication

Effective risk management requires collaboration and communication among cross-functional teams. Testers, developers, business analysts, and project managers collaborate to identify risks from different perspectives and ensure comprehensive coverage. Regular meetings, status updates, and risk review sessions facilitate transparent communication and alignment of testing activities with project goals.

3. Tools and Automation

Utilizing appropriate tools and automation enhances the efficiency and effectiveness of Risk-Based Testing. Test management tools facilitate risk identification, tracking, and reporting, enabling teams to manage risks systematically. Automation of repetitive test scenarios and regression testing frees up resources to focus on critical risk areas, accelerating the testing process without compromising quality.

4. Iterative Improvement

Continuous improvement is inherent in Risk-Based Testing. Throughout the project lifecycle, teams gather feedback, analyze testing outcomes, and refine their approach based on lessons learned. Retrospectives and post-mortem reviews provide valuable insights for optimizing future testing strategies and enhancing overall project delivery.

Challenges and Considerations

While Risk-Based Testing offers substantial benefits, its implementation is not without challenges. Key considerations include:

- **Risk Assessment Accuracy:** Ensuring the accuracy of risk assessments requires comprehensive data and expertise. Inaccurate risk prioritization can lead to ineffective testing strategies and overlooked vulnerabilities.
- **Changing Risk Landscape:** Project risks evolve over time due to changing requirements, market dynamics, and technological advancements. Continuous risk

monitoring and adaptation are essential to maintain relevance and effectiveness.

- **Resource Constraints:** Limited resources, including time and budget, can impact the extent to which Risk-Based Testing can be implemented. Prioritizing risks effectively helps optimize resource allocation and maximize testing efficiency.
- **Organizational Alignment:** Successful implementation of Risk-Based Testing necessitates organizational commitment and alignment. Stakeholder buy-in, supportive leadership, and a culture that values risk management are critical factors for sustainable adoption.

Risk-Based Testing represents a strategic approach to software testing that aligns testing efforts with project risks and objectives. By prioritizing testing based on risk severity and impact, teams can optimize resource allocation, enhance defect detection, and improve overall software quality. Successful implementation requires a structured risk management framework, effective collaboration, leveraging appropriate tools and automation, and a commitment to continuous improvement. While challenges exist, the benefits of Risk-Based Testing far outweigh the complexities, making it a valuable methodology for intermediate professionals looking to elevate their testing practices in today's competitive software development landscape.

Identifying and Assessing Risks

Risk-Based Testing (RBT) stands out as a pivotal strategy. It's not merely a practice but a structured approach that demands meticulous planning and execution. This method allows QA teams to prioritize their testing efforts based on the risks associated with the software under test (SUT). By identifying and assessing potential risks early in the development cycle, organizations can allocate their resources effectively, ensuring that critical functionalities are thoroughly tested while optimizing time and effort.

Understanding Risk-Based Testing

At its core, Risk-Based Testing revolves around the concept of risk assessment. Risk, in this context, refers to the likelihood of a defect occurring in a particular area of the software and the potential impact it could have on the end-users or the business. The goal is to focus testing efforts on areas of the software that are most critical, where defects would have the highest impact.

Key Principles of Risk-Based Testing

1. **Risk Identification**: The first step in Risk-Based Testing is to identify potential risks associated with the software. Risks can stem from various sources such as complex business logic, integration points, performance requirements, security vulnerabilities, and usability concerns. It requires a deep understanding of the project requirements, architecture, and potential usage scenarios.

2. **Risk Assessment**: Once risks are identified, they need to be assessed to understand their severity and likelihood. This assessment often involves collaboration between QA professionals, developers, business analysts, and other stakeholders. Risks are typically categorized based on their impact and probability, using qualitative or quantitative methods.

3. **Risk Mitigation Strategies**: After assessing risks, the next step is to devise mitigation strategies. This may involve adjusting the testing strategy to allocate more resources to high-risk areas, improving test coverage in critical functionalities, or implementing additional testing types such as security testing or performance testing.

4. **Continuous Monitoring and Adaptation**: Risk-Based Testing is not a one-time activity but a continuous process throughout the software development lifecycle. As the project progresses and new information becomes available, the risk landscape may evolve, requiring adjustments to the testing approach. Regular reviews and updates to the risk assessment are essential to ensure that testing efforts remain aligned with project priorities.

Benefits of Risk-Based Testing

Implementing Risk-Based Testing offers several benefits to organizations:

- **Efficient Resource Allocation**: By focusing testing efforts on high-risk areas, organizations can optimize their resources, ensuring that critical defects are identified and addressed early in the development cycle.

- **Early Defect Detection**: Testing high-risk areas early increases the likelihood of detecting critical defects before they impact the end-users, reducing the overall cost of quality.
- **Improved Test Coverage**: By prioritizing testing based on risk, organizations can achieve better test coverage in critical functionalities, ensuring that all essential scenarios are thoroughly tested.
- **Enhanced Stakeholder Confidence**: Stakeholders, including customers and business sponsors, gain confidence in the quality of the software when they see a proactive approach to risk management and testing.

Challenges in Implementing Risk-Based Testing

While Risk-Based Testing offers significant advantages, it is not without challenges:

- **Complexity in Risk Assessment**: Assessing risks accurately requires a deep understanding of the software, its intended use, and potential failure points. It can be challenging to quantify risks objectively, especially in complex systems.
- **Changing Risk Landscape**: Risks evolve over time as the project progresses, new requirements emerge, or external factors change. Maintaining an up-to-date risk assessment requires ongoing effort and collaboration.

- **Balancing Test Coverage**: Prioritizing testing based on risk can sometimes lead to neglecting lower-risk areas. It's essential to strike a balance between focusing on critical functionalities and ensuring comprehensive coverage across the entire application.
- **Resource Constraints**: Implementing Risk-Based Testing effectively may require additional resources, including skilled QA professionals, tools for risk assessment, and specialized testing environments.

Practical Implementation of Risk-Based Testing

To implement Risk-Based Testing effectively, organizations can follow these practical steps:

1. **Risk Identification Workshop**: Conduct workshops with stakeholders to brainstorm and identify potential risks based on project requirements, architecture, and user expectations.
2. **Risk Assessment and Prioritization**: Evaluate identified risks based on their impact and likelihood. Use risk matrices or other prioritization techniques to categorize risks and determine testing priorities.
3. **Testing Strategy Adjustment**: Tailor the testing strategy to allocate more resources to high-risk areas. Consider incorporating specific testing types such as exploratory testing, security testing, or performance testing based on identified risks.
4. **Continuous Monitoring and Reporting**: Regularly review and update the risk assessment throughout the software development lifecycle. Provide stakeholders

with transparent reports on risk status, testing progress, and identified defects.

Risk-Based Testing is a fundamental approach in the arsenal of modern software QA professionals. It provides a structured method to prioritize testing efforts based on the criticality of functionalities and potential impact of defects. By identifying and assessing risks early, organizations can optimize their testing resources, improve test coverage, and enhance overall software quality. While implementing Risk-Based Testing poses challenges, the benefits in terms of early defect detection, efficient resource allocation, and stakeholder confidence make it a worthwhile endeavor for any QA team committed to delivering high-quality software products.

Risk-Based Test Planning

Ensuring the quality of products has become synonymous with managing risks effectively. Among the many approaches available to achieve this, Risk-Based Testing (RBT) stands out as a methodical strategy that aligns testing efforts with potential risks to optimize resource allocation and enhance overall quality assurance.

Understanding Risk-Based Testing

At its core, Risk-Based Testing revolves around the principle of prioritization. Rather than adopting a one-size-fits-all testing strategy, RBT advocates for allocating testing efforts based on the perceived risks associated with the software under test. These risks can stem from various sources, including the impact of potential defects on end-users, critical functionalities of the application, regulatory requirements, and business priorities.

The rationale behind RBT lies in its ability to provide a structured approach to testing, where risks are identified, assessed, and managed proactively throughout the development lifecycle. By focusing testing efforts on areas with higher risk exposure, organizations can maximize the likelihood of detecting and mitigating critical defects early on, thereby reducing the overall cost of quality and improving time-to-market.

Key Elements of Risk-Based Test Planning

1. Risk Identification

The first step in implementing RBT is the identification of potential risks. This involves collaboration between stakeholders from different domains, including developers, testers, business analysts, and project managers. By leveraging their collective expertise, teams can identify risks associated with functionality, technology, performance, security, and usability aspects of the software.

2. Risk Assessment

Once risks are identified, the next step is to assess their potential impact and likelihood of occurrence. This assessment helps in prioritizing risks based on their severity and the probability of occurrence. Techniques such as Risk Matrix Analysis, Failure Mode and Effect Analysis (FMEA), and Expert Judgment are commonly used to evaluate and prioritize risks objectively.

3. Defining Test Strategy

Based on the prioritized risks, a tailored test strategy is formulated. This strategy outlines the testing objectives, scope, techniques, and deliverables aligned with mitigating identified risks. For instance, critical functionalities or modules prone to higher risks might undergo rigorous testing cycles, including regression testing, performance testing, security testing, and usability testing.

4. Test Design and Execution

With the test strategy in place, the focus shifts to test design and execution. Test cases are designed to verify the identified risks and their corresponding mitigation strategies. Testers ensure comprehensive coverage of high-risk areas while balancing efforts across the application. Test execution involves running test cases, capturing results, and validating against expected outcomes to uncover defects early in the development cycle.

5. Risk Monitoring and Control

Throughout the testing process, continuous monitoring of identified risks is essential. Test progress and results are analyzed to assess the effectiveness of risk mitigation measures and to identify any emerging risks. Feedback loops are established to refine test cases, adjust priorities, and update the test strategy as necessary to adapt to evolving project dynamics.

6. Reporting and Communication

Effective communication is critical in RBT to keep all stakeholders informed about the status of identified risks, testing progress, and overall quality metrics. Clear and concise reporting mechanisms, such as risk dashboards, test summary reports, and defect metrics, help in facilitating informed decision-making and maintaining transparency across the project team.

Benefits of Risk-Based Testing

The adoption of Risk-Based Testing offers several compelling benefits to organizations striving to deliver high-quality software products:

- **Optimized Resource Utilization:** By focusing testing efforts on high-risk areas, organizations can allocate resources more efficiently, thereby reducing costs associated with exhaustive testing across all functionalities.
- **Early Defect Detection:** RBT increases the likelihood of detecting critical defects early in the development lifecycle, minimizing rework and avoiding potential issues in production.
- **Enhanced Test Coverage:** Prioritizing testing based on risks ensures that critical functionalities and scenarios are thoroughly tested, leading to improved overall test coverage and confidence in product quality.
- **Improved Decision-Making:** Stakeholders can make informed decisions regarding release readiness and risk acceptance based on comprehensive risk and quality metrics provided by RBT practices.
- **Alignment with Business Goals:** RBT helps align testing efforts with business priorities, ensuring that

testing activities contribute directly to achieving organizational objectives and meeting customer expectations.

Challenges and Considerations

While Risk-Based Testing offers significant advantages, its successful implementation requires careful consideration of several factors:

- **Risk Assessment Accuracy:** The effectiveness of RBT hinges on the accuracy of risk assessment and prioritization. Inaccurate risk identification or assessment may lead to misallocation of testing efforts and inadequate risk coverage.
- **Continuous Adaptation:** RBT requires a flexible and adaptive approach to accommodate changes in project scope, requirements, and risk landscape throughout the software development lifecycle.
- **Expertise and Collaboration:** Effective implementation of RBT necessitates collaboration among cross-functional teams and domain experts to ensure comprehensive risk coverage and mitigation strategies.
- **Tool and Technology Support:** Leveraging appropriate tools and technologies for risk identification, assessment, and test management can streamline RBT processes and enhance overall efficiency.

Risk-Based Testing stands as a cornerstone of modern software quality assurance practices, offering a systematic approach to managing risks and enhancing testing efficiency. By prioritizing testing efforts based on identified risks, organizations can achieve significant improvements in product quality, resource utilization, and time-to-market. As software development continues to evolve, embracing Risk-Based Testing ensures that testing efforts remain aligned with business objectives and contribute effectively to delivering robust and reliable software solutions.

For software QA engineers and professionals aiming to elevate their testing practices, mastering the principles and methodologies of Risk-Based Testing is not just a recommendation but a strategic imperative in today's competitive landscape. By integrating RBT into their testing arsenal, professionals can not only mitigate risks effectively but also drive continuous improvement in software quality and stakeholder satisfaction.

Risk-Based Test Execution

Risk-Based Testing (RBT) stands out as a critical approach to ensuring that testing efforts are focused on areas of the software that are most likely to impact its functionality, reliability, and overall quality. At its core, RBT aligns testing activities with the identified risks associated with the software under test, thereby optimizing the allocation of resources and maximizing the effectiveness of testing efforts.

Understanding Risk-Based Testing

Risk-Based Testing is fundamentally rooted in the concept of risk management, which involves identifying potential risks, assessing their likelihood and impact, and then devising strategies to mitigate these risks. In the context of software QA, risks can manifest in various forms: from technical uncertainties in the implementation to business-critical functionalities that must perform flawlessly under diverse conditions.

The process begins with a comprehensive risk assessment, where potential risks to the software are identified and categorized based on their severity and probability of occurrence. This assessment is typically conducted collaboratively by QA engineers, developers, business analysts, and other stakeholders who possess domain-specific knowledge essential for accurate risk evaluation.

The Role of Risk-Based Test Execution

Once risks are identified and prioritized, the next logical step is to devise a testing strategy that reflects these priorities. This is where Risk-Based Test Execution (RBTE) comes into play. RBTE entails the planning, design, and execution of tests with a primary focus on mitigating the highest-priority risks identified during the risk assessment phase.

Key Components of Risk-Based Test Execution

1. **Risk Prioritization:** The cornerstone of RBTE lies in prioritizing tests based on the severity and likelihood of identified risks. Risks that have a higher potential impact on the software's performance or functionality are accorded greater testing emphasis.

2. **Test Case Design:** Test cases are designed to target specific risk scenarios. This involves creating test

scenarios that replicate conditions under which identified risks are likely to manifest. For instance, if a critical business function is susceptible to data input errors, test cases would be designed to validate the software's behavior under various erroneous input conditions.

3. **Test Execution Planning:** RBTE involves meticulous planning to ensure that testing efforts are aligned with project timelines and resource constraints. This includes determining the sequence of test execution, allocating resources such as test environments and testing tools, and establishing clear criteria for test completion and success.

4. **Continuous Risk Monitoring:** Throughout the test execution phase, QA teams continuously monitor identified risks to assess their evolving impact on the software. This iterative approach allows for timely adjustments to testing priorities and strategies in response to emerging risks or changes in project requirements.

Implementing Risk-Based Test Execution

Implementing RBTE effectively requires a structured approach and adherence to established best practices in software testing and risk management. Here are key steps involved in implementing RBTE:

Step 1: Risk Identification and Assessment

Begin by conducting a thorough risk assessment in collaboration with stakeholders from across the project team.

This involves identifying potential risks based on factors such as project complexity, technological dependencies, and business impact.

Step 2: Risk Prioritization

Once risks are identified, prioritize them based on their potential impact on the software's functionality, performance, and overall quality. Consider factors such as criticality of affected functionalities, likelihood of occurrence, and potential consequences of failure.

Step 3: Test Strategy Development

Develop a comprehensive test strategy that aligns with the identified risks. Define testing objectives, scope, and methodologies based on the prioritized risks. This may involve selecting appropriate testing techniques, such as exploratory testing for high-impact risks and regression testing for stability-related risks.

Step 4: Test Case Design and Preparation

Design test cases that specifically target high-priority risks identified during the risk assessment phase. Ensure that test cases are comprehensive, covering various scenarios and edge cases that could potentially expose vulnerabilities associated with identified risks.

Step 5: Test Execution and Monitoring

Execute tests according to the defined test strategy, focusing on validating software behavior under risk-specific conditions. Monitor test results closely to identify any deviations from expected outcomes and assess the impact of identified risks on the software's performance and functionality.

Step 6: Risk Mitigation and Reporting

Throughout the test execution phase, actively mitigate identified risks by addressing vulnerabilities and implementing necessary corrective actions. Prepare comprehensive test reports detailing test coverage, results, and observations related to risk mitigation efforts.

Step 7: Iterative Improvement

Continuously evaluate and refine the RBTE process based on insights gained from test results and stakeholder feedback. Identify opportunities for process improvement, such as enhancing risk assessment techniques, optimizing test case design, or refining test execution strategies.

Benefits of Risk-Based Test Execution

Implementing RBTE offers several tangible benefits to organizations engaged in software development and QA:

- **Focused Testing Efforts:** By prioritizing tests based on identified risks, RBTE ensures that testing efforts are directed towards areas of the software that are most susceptible to failure or performance degradation.
- **Optimized Resource Allocation:** RBTE enables efficient allocation of testing resources, including time, personnel, and infrastructure. This helps organizations maximize the return on investment in testing activities.

- **Early Defect Detection:** By targeting high-priority risks early in the development lifecycle, RBTE facilitates early detection and mitigation of defects, reducing the likelihood of costly rework and post-release issues.
- **Enhanced Stakeholder Confidence:** Stakeholders, including project sponsors, customers, and end-users, gain confidence in the software's quality and reliability due to focused testing efforts aimed at mitigating critical risks.

Challenges and Considerations

Despite its benefits, implementing RBTE poses several challenges and considerations that organizations must address:

- **Complex Risk Assessment:** Conducting accurate risk assessments requires a deep understanding of the software's technical and business context. Lack of domain-specific expertise or incomplete risk identification can undermine the effectiveness of RBTE.
- **Dynamic Risk Landscape:** The risk landscape can evolve rapidly due to changes in project scope, requirements, or external factors. Continuous monitoring and adaptation of testing strategies are essential to address emerging risks effectively.
- **Integration with Agile Practices:** RBTE must be seamlessly integrated with agile development practices, such as continuous integration and iterative delivery cycles. This requires collaboration and coordination

between QA teams, developers, and other project stakeholders.

- **Measurement of Effectiveness:** Assessing the effectiveness of RBTE requires robust metrics and performance indicators. Organizations should define clear criteria for evaluating test coverage, defect detection rates, and overall risk mitigation success.

Risk-Based Test Execution represents a strategic approach to software testing that aligns testing efforts with identified risks, thereby enhancing the effectiveness and efficiency of QA activities. By prioritizing tests based on the severity and likelihood of potential risks, organizations can optimize resource allocation, improve defect detection rates, and ultimately deliver higher quality software to end-users.

Successful implementation of RBTE requires a structured approach to risk assessment, meticulous test planning, and continuous monitoring of identified risks throughout the software development lifecycle. By embracing RBTE principles and integrating them with established best practices in software testing and risk management, organizations can mitigate project risks proactively and achieve their quality assurance objectives with confidence.

Chapter Six

Advanced Performance Testing

Performance Test Scripting Techniques

Performance testing stands as a cornerstone of modern software quality assurance, ensuring applications can handle expected workloads efficiently and reliably. Within this discipline lies a crucial component: performance test scripting techniques. These techniques encompass a spectrum of methodologies and practices aimed at crafting scripts that simulate real-world usage scenarios, thereby evaluating system performance under various conditions. For intermediate professionals in software QA engineering, mastering these advanced scripting techniques is essential for enhancing the effectiveness and precision of performance tests.

Understanding Performance Test Scripting

At its core, performance test scripting involves the creation of scripts that emulate user interactions with an application. These scripts are designed to simulate typical user behaviors and system interactions, such as logging in, browsing content, making transactions, and handling data. The goal is to replicate real-world scenarios accurately, ensuring that the performance metrics gathered during testing reflect actual user experiences.

Key Components of Effective Performance Test Scripts

1. **Scripting Languages and Tools**:
   - **Selection**: Choosing the right scripting language and tools is critical. Common choices include scripting languages like JMeter, Gatling, and LoadRunner, each offering unique capabilities suited to different testing requirements.
   - **Customization**: Tailoring scripts to match specific application architectures and technologies ensures realistic simulation of user activities.
2. **Scenario Design**:
   - **Realism**: Scripts should reflect real-world usage patterns, encompassing variations in user behaviors, data inputs, and navigation paths.
   - **Edge Cases**: Incorporating edge cases and stress scenarios tests system resilience and performance under adverse conditions.
3. **Data Management**:
   - **Parameterization**: Dynamic data handling through parameterization ensures variability in input values, reflecting diverse user inputs and data volumes.

- **Data Correlation**: Managing session-specific data and correlations between requests accurately reproduces session continuity and behavior.

Advanced Techniques in Performance Test Scripting

1. **Protocol Level Scripting**:
   - **HTTP/S and Beyond**: Scripting at the protocol level allows deep inspection of network interactions, enabling precise control over request and response handling.
   - **Binary Protocols**: Handling binary protocols requires specialized scripting techniques to parse and manipulate data streams effectively.
2. **JavaScript and Browser-based Scripts**:
   - **Browser Emulation**: Using tools like Selenium for scripting allows simulation of complex user interactions within web applications.
   - **Client-Side Performance**: Measuring and optimizing client-side performance metrics through JavaScript-based scripts enhances end-user experience assessment.
3. **API and Microservices Testing**:
   - **RESTful APIs**: Scripting for API endpoints involves crafting requests that mimic service

consumer behavior, focusing on throughput, response times, and error handling.

- **Message Brokers**: Testing message-oriented middleware requires scripting techniques capable of managing asynchronous message flows and validating message integrity.

Implementation Best Practices

1. **Modular Script Design**:
    - **Reusable Components**: Modular scripts facilitate code reuse and maintenance, enhancing scalability across different test scenarios.
    - **Parameter Management**: Centralized parameterization and configuration management streamline script updates and ensure consistency.
2. **Performance Metrics Integration**:
    - **Metric Collection**: Incorporating metrics like response times, throughput, and resource utilization within scripts enables real-time performance monitoring.
    - **Analysis and Reporting**: Automated metric analysis and report generation provide actionable insights into system performance trends and bottlenecks.

3. **Scalability and Load Distribution**:
    - **Virtual User Simulation**: Scaling scripts to simulate thousands of concurrent users requires load distribution techniques to distribute virtual user load effectively.
    - **Cloud-based Testing**: Leveraging cloud infrastructure for distributed load generation ensures scalability and replicability across geographically diverse user bases.

Challenges and Considerations

1. **Dynamic Environments**:
    - **Environment Variability**: Adapting scripts to varying test environments (e.g., development, staging, production) requires robust configuration management and environment-specific parameterization.
    - **Security and Compliance**: Ensuring scripts adhere to security protocols and regulatory requirements minimizes data exposure risks during performance testing.
2. **Script Maintenance and Version Control**:
    - **Versioning**: Implementing version control for scripts facilitates collaboration among team members and ensures traceability of script changes over time.

- **Continuous Integration**: Integrating performance test scripts into CI/CD pipelines automates testing workflows, promoting early detection of performance regressions.

Future Trends and Innovations

1. **AI and Machine Learning in Performance Testing**:
   - **Predictive Analytics**: AI-driven performance testing tools offer predictive analytics capabilities for anticipating system behavior under future loads.
   - **Self-Healing Systems**: Autonomous test script optimization and adaptive load balancing based on machine learning algorithms enhance testing efficiency and accuracy.
2. **Containerization and Microservices Architecture**:
   - **Orchestration**: Container-based orchestration tools like Kubernetes enable scalable deployment and management of performance test environments.
   - **Service Mesh Integration**: Testing within service mesh architectures requires scripting techniques that accommodate complex service interactions and observability needs.

Mastering advanced performance test scripting techniques empowers intermediate professionals in software QA engineering to conduct comprehensive performance assessments that align closely with real-world usage scenarios. By employing appropriate scripting languages, designing realistic test scenarios, and integrating robust performance metrics, QA engineers can ensure the reliability, scalability, and responsiveness of software applications in diverse operational contexts. Embracing emerging trends such as AI-driven testing and containerized deployment further equips professionals to stay ahead in an ever-evolving landscape of software performance testing.

In conclusion, as software systems continue to grow in complexity and scale, the role of advanced performance testing and meticulous script crafting becomes increasingly indispensable in guaranteeing optimal user experiences and operational excellence.

Performance Monitoring and Analysis

Performance testing stands at the forefront of ensuring the robustness and reliability of software systems in today's digital age. As software QA engineers delve deeper into the intricacies of performance testing, they encounter challenges that demand advanced techniques in performance monitoring and analysis. This article explores the pivotal role of performance monitoring and analysis in software quality assurance, emphasizing its technical nuances and practical applications.

Understanding Performance Monitoring

Performance monitoring is the systematic process of observing and evaluating key metrics of a software application under various conditions. It serves as the first line of defense against performance bottlenecks and inefficiencies that could undermine user experience or system stability. Effective performance monitoring relies on a combination of tools, methodologies, and skilled analysis to capture real-time data and trends accurately.

At its core, performance monitoring involves the continuous collection of metrics such as response times, throughput rates, error rates, and resource utilization (CPU, memory, disk I/O). These metrics provide crucial insights into the health and efficiency of the software system. Modern monitoring tools offer a plethora of features including customizable dashboards, alerting mechanisms, and integration with other software development lifecycle (SDLC) tools.

The Role of Performance Analysis

Performance analysis complements monitoring by interpreting the collected data to identify patterns, anomalies, and potential areas for optimization. It involves deep dives into performance metrics to uncover root causes of issues and to validate system behaviors against predefined benchmarks or service level agreements (SLAs). Performance analysts employ various techniques such as statistical analysis, correlation studies, and profiling to extract meaningful insights from raw performance data.

An essential aspect of performance analysis is the ability to distinguish between symptoms and underlying causes of performance degradation. This requires a blend of technical expertise, analytical skills, and domain knowledge to contextualize performance metrics within the specific architecture and usage patterns of the software application.

Advanced Techniques in Performance Testing

As software systems grow in complexity and scale, traditional performance testing approaches may prove inadequate. Advanced performance testing techniques go beyond mere load testing to encompass sophisticated methodologies such as:

1. **Stress Testing**: Simulating extreme load conditions to determine system breaking points and scalability limits.

2. **Endurance Testing**: Evaluating system performance over prolonged periods to assess stability and resource leakage.

3. **Spike Testing**: Subjecting the system to sudden, sharp increases in load to gauge its ability to handle unexpected surges in user traffic.

Each of these techniques requires meticulous planning, execution, and analysis to derive meaningful conclusions about system performance under varying conditions.

Challenges and Considerations

Despite its importance, effective performance monitoring and analysis present several challenges for software QA engineers:

1. **Tool Selection**: Choosing the right monitoring tools that align with the technology stack and scalability requirements of the application.

2. **Data Overload**: Managing large volumes of performance data and distinguishing between actionable insights and noise.

3. **Real-time Analysis**: Ensuring timely analysis and response to performance issues to minimize impact on end users.

4. **Interpretation Complexity**: Interpreting performance metrics in the context of changing user behaviors, application updates, and infrastructure changes.

Addressing these challenges requires a holistic approach that integrates technical expertise with strategic planning and continuous improvement initiatives within the QA process.

Best Practices and Recommendations

To maximize the effectiveness of performance testing, software QA engineers should consider adopting the following best practices:

1. **Establish Clear Performance Goals**: Define measurable performance objectives and benchmarks aligned with business requirements.

2. **Continuous Monitoring**: Implement proactive monitoring strategies to detect performance deviations early and preemptively.

3. **Automated Analysis**: Leverage automation tools for data collection, analysis, and reporting to streamline the performance testing lifecycle.

4. **Collaborative Approach**: Foster collaboration between development, QA, and operations teams to promote a culture of performance awareness and accountability.

5. **Iterative Optimization**: Continuously refine performance testing strategies based on feedback, emerging trends, and evolving user demands.

By embracing these best practices, organizations can cultivate a proactive approach to performance testing that enhances software quality, improves user satisfaction, and mitigates risks associated with performance-related issues.

Advanced performance testing, particularly through meticulous monitoring and insightful analysis, serves as a cornerstone of effective software quality assurance. By leveraging sophisticated tools and methodologies, software QA engineers can uncover hidden performance bottlenecks, optimize system efficiency, and ultimately deliver a superior user experience. As technology evolves, the role of performance monitoring and analysis will continue to expand, necessitating a proactive and adaptive approach to meet the dynamic challenges of modern software development.

Through continuous refinement of techniques and a commitment to excellence, software QA professionals can uphold the highest standards of performance testing, ensuring that software applications not only meet but exceed expectations in an increasingly competitive digital landscape.

Advanced Load Testing Strategies

Performance testing stands as a critical pillar in ensuring the robustness and reliability of applications under varying workloads. Advanced load testing, a subset of performance testing, delves deeper into the intricacies of simulating real-world usage scenarios to assess system behavior and performance metrics under stress. This article explores advanced load testing strategies, aiming to equip intermediate professionals with nuanced techniques and methodologies essential for optimizing software performance.

Understanding Advanced Load Testing

Load testing, at its core, involves subjecting an application to simulated workloads to evaluate its response and stability. Advanced load testing extends beyond basic scenarios by incorporating complex use cases and stress conditions, reflecting actual user interactions and system behaviors at scale. The primary objective shifts from mere response times to identifying bottlenecks, scalability limits, and resource utilization patterns under extreme loads.

Key Components of Advanced Load Testing

1. Scenario Design

Advanced load testing begins with meticulous scenario design, which defines the user behaviors, transaction flows, and workload distributions that the test will simulate. Unlike simpler load tests, advanced scenarios may involve multiple user profiles, each executing distinct actions concurrently. For instance, an e-commerce application might simulate simultaneous browsing, shopping cart updates, and checkout processes across a spectrum of user types (e.g., guest users, registered users, admin accounts).

2. Realistic Workload Modeling

Accurate workload modeling is crucial for effective advanced load testing. This involves analyzing production data or user behavior patterns to create realistic load profiles. Tools like Apache JMeter, LoadRunner, and Gatling are employed to generate varying loads, mimicking peak traffic conditions or sudden spikes in user activity. Advanced techniques include ramp-up schedules, where load is gradually increased, and spike tests to evaluate system resilience under sudden load surges.

3. Protocol Level Testing

Going beyond HTTP-based interactions, advanced load testing often incorporates protocol-level testing for applications using diverse communication protocols (e.g., TCP/IP, SOAP, REST). This approach enables detailed analysis of network-level performance metrics such as latency, throughput, and packet loss under heavy loads. Tools supporting protocol-level testing provide deeper insights into how network conditions impact application performance and scalability.

4. Distributed Testing

To simulate geographically dispersed user bases, distributed load testing distributes virtual users across multiple test environments or geographies. This approach assesses the application's ability to maintain performance consistency and data integrity across different regions. Advanced load testing frameworks allow for seamless coordination and synchronization among distributed test agents, ensuring accurate load distribution and cohesive test results analysis.

5. Dynamic Parameterization

Dynamic parameterization involves injecting dynamic data elements (e.g., session IDs, timestamps, user tokens) into test scenarios to emulate realistic user interactions. Advanced load testing tools support parameterization techniques that facilitate dynamic data generation and correlation across concurrent user sessions. This ensures that each virtual user behaves uniquely, preventing caching or session-related issues that might skew test results.

6. Performance Metrics and Analysis

Effective performance testing hinges on comprehensive metrics collection and analysis. Advanced load testing incorporates a broad array of performance metrics beyond response times, including CPU utilization, memory consumption, database query performance, and server-side resource allocation. These metrics provide holistic insights into system health, identifying performance bottlenecks and areas for optimization across different layers of the application stack.

Advanced Strategies in Action

Case Study: Scaling a Video Streaming Service

Consider a video streaming service preparing for a global product launch. Advanced load testing strategies are essential to ensure seamless user experiences across diverse devices and regions. Here's how advanced load testing principles can be applied:

- **Global Load Distribution:** Simulate simultaneous video streaming requests from various geographic locations using distributed load testing.
- **Device Diversity:** Test application performance across different devices (e.g., smartphones, smart TVs)

to validate adaptive streaming capabilities and device-specific optimizations.

- **Real-Time Analytics:** Implement real-time monitoring and analytics to detect performance anomalies (e.g., buffering issues, playback failures) and adjust load testing parameters dynamically.

Best Practices: Optimizing Enterprise Resource Planning (ERP) Systems

For ERP systems handling complex business processes, advanced load testing is instrumental in maintaining operational efficiency and data integrity. Key strategies include:

- **Business Process Simulation:** Model end-to-end business processes (e.g., order processing, inventory management) to simulate realistic user workflows and transaction volumes.
- **Peak Load Validation:** Validate ERP system scalability by stress testing peak transaction volumes and concurrent user activities during critical business cycles (e.g., month-end financial closures, holiday sales periods).
- **Database Performance:** Evaluate database query performance and indexing strategies to optimize data retrieval times and ensure efficient data processing under load.

Advanced load testing represents a pivotal stage in the software quality assurance lifecycle, enabling organizations to proactively identify and mitigate performance bottlenecks before deployment. By adopting sophisticated strategies such as realistic workload modeling, protocol-level testing, and dynamic parameterization, QA professionals can conduct thorough performance assessments that align with real-world usage scenarios. Embracing advanced load testing not only enhances application reliability and scalability but also fosters user confidence and satisfaction in today's competitive digital landscape.

Performance Tuning and Optimization

Within the expansive realm of software development, ensuring the quality and reliability of a product is paramount. Among the various techniques employed to achieve this goal, Regression Testing stands out as a cornerstone practice. It is a meticulous process that involves retesting previously validated functionalities to ensure that recent changes or enhancements haven't adversely affected them. Within this practice lies a crucial aspect: Regression Test Automation.

Chapter Seven

Advanced Security Testing

Secure Coding Practices

Performance testing is essential in software quality assurance to ensure a system handles expected loads and performance levels. It goes beyond identifying bottlenecks, aiming to ensure software operates optimally under various conditions and workloads. Advanced performance testing involves a systematic approach to performance tuning and optimization, requiring deep knowledge of system architecture, detailed planning, execution of testing strategies, and effective communication with development and operations teams.

Understanding System Architecture

The first step in advanced performance testing is thoroughly understanding the system architecture. This includes hardware specifications, software environment, network configurations, and component interactions. Knowledge of the architecture helps identify potential performance bottlenecks and areas needing optimization. For instance, knowing whether the system is monolithic or microservices-based influences the testing strategy and tools used.

Planning and Strategy

Effective performance testing starts with comprehensive planning. Define clear objectives for the performance tests. Are you testing for response time, throughput, scalability, or resource utilization? Once objectives are set, create a detailed test plan that includes the following elements:

1. **Test Scenarios**: Outline various scenarios to be tested, including peak load, average load, and stress conditions.

2. **Metrics to Measure**: Identify key performance indicators (KPIs) such as response time, transaction rate, error rate, and resource utilization.

3. **Tools and Environment**: Select appropriate performance testing tools and set up a testing environment that closely mimics the production environment. Tools like Apache JMeter, LoadRunner, and Gatling are commonly used for performance testing.

4. **Test Data**: Prepare realistic test data reflecting actual usage patterns, including data size, volume, and variability.

5. **Baseline Performance**: Establish a baseline by running initial tests. This serves as a reference for measuring improvements and identifying regressions.

Execution and Monitoring

Executing performance tests involves running the planned scenarios and monitoring system performance. During this phase, it's crucial to collect and analyze data in real-time to identify issues quickly. Use monitoring tools to track CPU usage, memory consumption, disk I/O, and network activity. Essential steps during execution include:

1. **Simulating Load**: Use performance testing tools to simulate the expected load, including user numbers and interaction types.
2. **Monitoring**: Continuously monitor system performance using tools like New Relic, Dynatrace, or Grafana to gain insights into system behavior under load.
3. **Logging and Reporting**: Collect logs and generate reports detailing system performance metrics. These reports are crucial for identifying trends and pinpointing improvement areas.

Analyzing Results

After executing tests, analyze the results to identify performance issues. Look for patterns and correlations in the data. For instance, if response time increases significantly under load, investigate whether it correlates with high CPU usage or memory consumption. Use statistical analysis to understand the significance of observed performance metrics. Key focus areas include:

1. **Bottleneck Identification**: Determine the root cause of performance issues, such as inefficient code, resource contention, or hardware limitations.
2. **Resource Utilization**: Analyze how efficiently the system uses resources, identifying overutilized or underutilized components.

3. **Scalability**: Assess the system's ability to scale, including both horizontal scaling (adding more machines) and vertical scaling (adding more resources to existing machines).

Performance Tuning

Once performance issues are identified, the next step is performance tuning, which involves making changes to optimize performance. Tuning can occur at various levels of the system:

1. **Application Level**: Optimize code to improve efficiency, including refactoring inefficient algorithms, reducing database query complexity, and optimizing memory usage.

2. **Database Level**: Enhance database performance by indexing, query optimization, and ensuring efficient database schema design.

3. **Server Configuration**: Adjust server settings to improve performance, such as tweaking thread pools, adjusting garbage collection settings, or optimizing network settings.

4. **Load Balancing**: Implement or optimize load balancing to distribute the workload evenly across servers.

Continuous Optimization

Performance tuning is an ongoing process. As the system evolves, new performance issues may arise. Incorporating performance testing into the continuous integration and continuous deployment (CI/CD) pipeline is essential. This ensures performance is tested with every code change, and any regressions are detected early.

1. **Automated Testing**: Integrate performance tests into the CI/CD pipeline. Automated tests can be triggered with every build to ensure performance standards are maintained.

2. **Regular Monitoring**: Continuously monitor system performance in production using real user monitoring (RUM) tools to gather performance data from actual users.

3. **Feedback Loop**: Establish a feedback loop where performance issues detected in production are fed back into the development cycle for resolution.

Best Practices for Performance Tuning

Adopting best practices in performance tuning can significantly enhance optimization efforts. Some best practices include:

1. **Incremental Changes**: Make incremental changes and measure their impact to isolate the effect of each change and understand its contribution to performance improvement.

2. **Load Testing in Isolation**: Test components in isolation to identify their performance characteristics and understand how each contributes to overall system performance.

3. **User-Centric Testing**: Focus on the end-user experience. Performance metrics should reflect the user's perspective, such as page load time and responsiveness.

4. **Documentation**: Maintain detailed documentation of performance issues, tuning steps, and their impact. This knowledge base can be invaluable for future performance tuning efforts.

Case Study: Practical Application of Performance Tuning

To illustrate performance tuning, consider an e-commerce application experiencing slow response times during peak traffic. Initial performance testing revealed the application struggled to handle more than 1,000 concurrent users, with response times exceeding 5 seconds.

1. **Initial Analysis**: Identified several bottlenecks, including high database contention and application servers running out of memory under load.

2. **Database Optimization**: Optimized database queries by indexing frequently accessed columns and optimizing complex joins, reducing database response time by 40%.

3. **Code Optimization**: Profiled the application code, revealing inefficient algorithms in the checkout process. Refactoring these algorithms reduced response time by an additional 20%.

4. **Server Configuration**: Reconfigured application servers to better handle the load, including increasing JVM heap size and optimizing thread pool settings.

5. **Load Balancing**: Implemented a load balancer to distribute traffic evenly across multiple servers, preventing any single server from becoming a bottleneck.

After these optimizations, the performance tests were rerun. The application could now handle 5,000 concurrent users with response times under 2 seconds. This significant improvement not only enhanced user satisfaction but also increased the overall application capacity.

Advanced performance testing, tuning, and optimization are crucial for ensuring software systems perform efficiently under various conditions. It requires a methodical approach, starting from understanding the system architecture, planning and executing performance tests, analyzing the results, and implementing targeted optimizations. Continuous monitoring and integration of performance testing into the development cycle ensure performance standards are maintained as the system evolves. By following best practices and learning from real-world applications, QA engineers can significantly enhance the performance and reliability of their software systems.

Threat Modeling

In today's interconnected environment, the importance of secure coding practices cannot be overstated. With cyber threats evolving at an alarming pace, the responsibility falls on software quality assurance (QA) professionals to ensure not only functionality and performance but also to rigorously test for security vulnerabilities. Advanced security testing is a crucial component of this effort, emphasizing the need for meticulous attention to secure coding practices.

Understanding Secure Coding Practices

Secure coding practices are a set of guidelines and best practices aimed at minimizing the vulnerabilities within software applications. These practices are integral to the development lifecycle, ensuring that security is embedded at every stage from design to deployment. Secure coding focuses on identifying and mitigating potential security flaws that could be exploited by malicious actors.

Common Security Vulnerabilities

To appreciate the importance of secure coding, it's essential to understand the common vulnerabilities that plague software applications. The Open Web Application Security Project (OWASP) provides a comprehensive list of these vulnerabilities, commonly referred to as the OWASP Top Ten. They include:

1. **Injection Flaws**: Occur when untrusted data is sent to an interpreter as part of a command or query.

2. **Broken Authentication**: Involves flaws in the authentication process that allow attackers to compromise passwords, keys, or session tokens.

3. **Sensitive Data Exposure**: Happens when applications fail to adequately protect sensitive

information, such as credit card data or personal information.

4. **XML External Entities (XXE)**: Occur when an application processes XML input with a reference to an external entity.
5. **Broken Access Control**: Allows users to act outside their intended permissions.
6. **Security Misconfiguration**: Involves improper configuration of security settings.
7. **Cross-Site Scripting (XSS)**: Occurs when an application includes untrusted data in a new webpage without proper validation or escaping.
8. **Insecure Deserialization**: Involves deserializing untrusted data, which can lead to remote code execution.
9. **Using Components with Known Vulnerabilities**: Happens when applications use libraries, frameworks, or other software modules with known security flaws.
10. **Insufficient Logging and Monitoring**: Fails to detect or respond to potential security breaches.

Principles of Secure Coding

Secure coding is grounded in several fundamental principles, each designed to mitigate the risks posed by these vulnerabilities:

Least Privilege

This principle dictates that a system should grant only the necessary permissions required for an operation to reduce the potential damage from a security breach. Implementing least privilege involves restricting user permissions and ensuring that applications operate with the minimum level of access needed.

Defense in Depth

This strategy involves implementing multiple layers of security controls and measures. If one layer is compromised, subsequent layers continue to provide protection. Defense in depth can include a combination of firewalls, intrusion detection systems, encryption, and application-level security measures.

Input Validation

Input validation ensures that all data entering a system is verified for accuracy and integrity. This can prevent injection attacks and other malicious input-related exploits. Effective input validation includes both client-side and server-side checks to ensure robustness.

Secure Error Handling

Proper error handling prevents attackers from gaining insight into the system through error messages. Secure error handling ensures that errors do not reveal sensitive information and that the application continues to operate securely even in the event of an error.

Techniques for Secure Coding

Implementing secure coding practices requires a combination of techniques and tools designed to identify and address potential security issues:

Static Code Analysis

Static code analysis involves examining source code without executing it. This technique can identify security vulnerabilities, coding errors, and deviations from best practices. Tools like SonarQube, Checkmarx, and Fortify can automate static code analysis, providing detailed reports on potential issues.

Dynamic Analysis

Unlike static analysis, dynamic analysis examines the behavior of an application during execution. This technique can identify vulnerabilities that arise from the interaction of various components in a running system. Tools such as OWASP ZAP and Burp Suite are commonly used for dynamic analysis, simulating attacks to uncover potential weaknesses.

Code Reviews

Peer code reviews involve having other developers examine code for security flaws and adherence to best practices. Regular code reviews can catch issues early in the development process, ensuring that secure coding practices are followed consistently.

Threat Modeling

Threat modeling involves identifying potential threats and vulnerabilities during the design phase of a project. By anticipating possible attack vectors, developers can design more secure systems from the outset. Tools like Microsoft's Threat Modeling Tool can facilitate this process, helping teams to visualize and mitigate threats effectively.

Secure Coding Guidelines

Adhering to established secure coding guidelines is critical for minimizing vulnerabilities. Organizations like OWASP and CERT provide comprehensive guidelines that cover a wide range of programming languages and environments. Key guidelines include:

1. **Avoiding Hardcoded Credentials**: Storing credentials in source code can lead to significant security breaches. Use secure storage mechanisms such as environment variables or secure vaults.

2. **Implementing Secure Session Management**: Ensure that session tokens are generated securely and transmitted over secure channels. Implement mechanisms to detect and prevent session hijacking.

3. **Using Parameterized Queries**: To prevent SQL injection, use parameterized queries instead of concatenating user input with SQL statements.

4. **Sanitizing Data Input**: Ensure all user inputs are sanitized and validated. Use frameworks and libraries that provide built-in sanitization functions.

5. **Encrypting Sensitive Data**: Use strong encryption algorithms to protect sensitive data both at rest and in transit. Ensure encryption keys are managed securely.

6. **Regularly Updating Dependencies**: Keep all software dependencies up to date to avoid vulnerabilities in third-party libraries.

Integrating Security Testing into CI/CD Pipelines

To ensure that secure coding practices are consistently applied, integrate security testing into Continuous Integration/Continuous Deployment (CI/CD) pipelines. This integration allows for automated security checks at every stage of development, ensuring that security is an ongoing process rather than a one-time effort.

Automated Security Testing Tools

Several tools can be integrated into CI/CD pipelines to automate security testing:

1. **Static Application Security Testing (SAST)**: Tools like SonarQube and Checkmarx can be configured to run static analysis during the build process, identifying security flaws early.

2. **Dynamic Application Security Testing (DAST)**: Tools like OWASP ZAP and Burp Suite can perform dynamic analysis on deployed applications, identifying runtime vulnerabilities.

3. **Software Composition Analysis (SCA)**: Tools like Snyk and WhiteSource can analyze dependencies and

third-party libraries for known vulnerabilities, ensuring that all components are secure.

Case Study: Secure Coding in Practice

Consider a software development team working on a web application for financial transactions. The team adopts secure coding practices from the outset, integrating static and dynamic analysis tools into their CI/CD pipeline. They follow OWASP guidelines, conducting regular code reviews and threat modeling sessions.

During development, the static analysis tool identifies a potential SQL injection vulnerability. The team addresses this by implementing parameterized queries. Dynamic analysis later uncovers a session fixation issue, which is resolved by enhancing session management practices.

By adhering to secure coding principles and leveraging automated tools, the team significantly reduces the risk of security breaches. Regular updates to dependencies and continuous monitoring ensure that the application remains secure even as new threats emerge.

Secure coding practices are an essential aspect of advanced security testing. By understanding common vulnerabilities, adhering to fundamental principles, and leveraging both manual and automated techniques, QA professionals can significantly enhance the security posture of their applications. Integrating security testing into CI/CD pipelines ensures that security is an ongoing concern, embedded into every stage of the development lifecycle. Through diligent application of secure coding practices, teams can safeguard their software against the continuously changing landscape of cyber threats, ensuring robust and resilient applications.

Penetration Testing

In software quality assurance, advanced security testing is crucial. Among the various techniques, threat modeling stands out as a fundamental approach for identifying, assessing, and addressing potential security threats throughout the software development lifecycle. By predicting potential vulnerabilities, threat modeling helps to reinforce applications against malicious activities.

The Importance of Threat Modeling

Threat modeling is a systematic process for identifying and managing security risks. It involves understanding the application, pinpointing potential threats, and devising measures to mitigate these threats. The main goal is to prioritize threats based on their risk levels and develop strategies to counter them before they can be exploited.

This proactive method contrasts with reactive approaches, such as penetration testing, which typically occur later in the development cycle. By incorporating threat modeling early and throughout the development process, security becomes an integral part of the software's design and implementation, rather than an afterthought.

Key Steps in Threat Modeling

1. **Define Security Objectives**: Start by understanding the purpose of the application and the data it handles.

Establish what constitutes a security breach for the application. Security objectives should align with business goals and regulatory requirements.

2. **Application Decomposition**: Break the application into its components to understand data flows and interactions. Identify assets (e.g., databases, files, network interfaces) and trust boundaries (points where data moves between different zones of control).

3. **Identify Threats**: Use frameworks like STRIDE (Spoofing, Tampering, Repudiation, Information Disclosure, Denial of Service, Elevation of Privilege) to systematically identify potential threats. This involves analyzing each component and data flow for vulnerabilities.

4. **Prioritize Threats**: Not all threats are created equal. Use risk assessment techniques to prioritize threats based on their potential impact and likelihood. Consider factors like the value of the asset, ease of exploitation, and potential damage.

5. **Mitigation Strategies**: Develop strategies to mitigate identified threats. This can include architectural changes, adding security controls, and defining secure coding practices. Document these strategies and ensure they are implemented and tested.

6. **Validation and Testing**: Validate the effectiveness of the mitigation strategies through security testing. This includes code reviews, automated security testing tools, and manual testing. Update the threat model as necessary based on the testing results.

Tools and Techniques

Several tools and techniques aid the threat modeling process:

- **Data Flow Diagrams (DFDs)**: Visual representations of data flow within an application. They help identify trust boundaries and potential points of attack.
- **Automated Tools**: Tools like Microsoft Threat Modeling Tool and OWASP Threat Dragon facilitate the creation and analysis of threat models. They help automate the identification of threats based on predefined patterns.
- **Frameworks and Standards**: Frameworks like STRIDE and standards like NIST SP 800-154 provide structured methodologies for threat modeling. These frameworks ensure consistency and thoroughness in the threat modeling process.

Best Practices

To maximize the effectiveness of threat modeling, consider the following best practices:

- **Integrate Early**: Incorporate threat modeling from the early stages of development. This ensures that security considerations influence design decisions from the outset.
- **Iterate Regularly**: Threat modeling is not a one-time activity. Regularly update the threat model as the application evolves, new features are added, or the threat environment changes.

- **Collaborate**: Involve cross-functional teams, including developers, testers, architects, and business stakeholders. Diverse perspectives help identify a broader range of threats and ensure that mitigation strategies are practical and effective.

- **Educate and Train**: Provide ongoing training to development and QA teams on security principles and threat modeling techniques. A security-aware culture enhances the overall effectiveness of threat modeling.

- **Leverage Automation**: Use automated tools to support the threat modeling process. Automation helps ensure consistency, reduces manual effort, and allows teams to focus on complex and high-priority threats.

Challenges and Considerations

While threat modeling offers significant benefits, it also presents challenges:

- **Complexity**: Large and complex systems can make threat modeling a daunting task. Break down the system into manageable components and focus on critical areas to mitigate this complexity.

- **Evolving Threat Landscape**: The threat landscape is continuously evolving, with new vulnerabilities and attack vectors emerging. Stay updated with the latest security trends and incorporate this knowledge into your threat models.

- **Balancing Security and Usability**: Implementing security measures can sometimes impact usability. Strive for a balance where security controls do not hinder the user experience. Engage with UX designers to find optimal solutions.

- **Resource Constraints**: Threat modeling can be resource-intensive. Prioritize critical components and high-risk areas to make the best use of available resources.

Case Study: Implementing Threat Modeling in a Financial Application

Consider a financial application handling sensitive customer data. Implementing threat modeling in this context involves several steps:

1. **Define Security Objectives**: Protect customer data, ensure transaction integrity, and comply with regulations like GDPR and PCI DSS.

2. **Application Decomposition**: Break down the application into modules such as authentication, transaction processing, and data storage. Identify assets like the database storing customer information and trust boundaries, such as the interface between the application and external payment gateways.

3. **Identify Threats**: Use the STRIDE framework to identify threats. For instance, spoofing threats in the authentication module, tampering threats in transaction processing, and information disclosure threats in data storage.

4. **Prioritize Threats**: Assess the impact and likelihood of each threat. For example, an attacker gaining

unauthorized access to customer data has a high impact and likelihood, thus a high priority.

5. **Mitigation Strategies**: Implement multi-factor authentication to mitigate spoofing, use cryptographic techniques to ensure data integrity, and encrypt sensitive data at rest and in transit.

6. **Validation and Testing**: Conduct security testing, including penetration testing and code reviews, to validate the effectiveness of the mitigation strategies. Update the threat model based on the testing results and refine the strategies as needed.

Threat modeling is a critical component of advanced security testing, providing a structured approach to identify, assess, and mitigate potential security threats. By integrating threat modeling early and iterating regularly, organizations can build more secure applications and protect against evolving threats. Effective threat modeling requires collaboration, ongoing education, and the use of appropriate tools and frameworks. Despite the challenges, the benefits of a robust threat modeling process far outweigh the effort, contributing significantly to the security and resilience of software systems.

Security Testing in DevSecOps

Integrating security testing within DevSecOps has become essential in modern software development. As the traditional silos between development, security, and operations teams dissolve, incorporating security as a core component of the development pipeline is not merely a best practice—it is a necessity. This shift requires a deep understanding of advanced security testing techniques and the implementation of these practices in a continuous integration/continuous deployment (CI/CD) environment.

The Imperative of Security in DevSecOps

DevSecOps is a natural evolution of DevOps, embedding security into every phase of the software development lifecycle (SDLC). This integration ensures that security is not an afterthought but an ongoing concern addressed from the initial design through to deployment and maintenance. The goal is to identify and mitigate vulnerabilities as early as possible, reducing the cost and impact of security issues.

Continuous Security: Automated and Integrated

Incorporating security into the CI/CD pipeline necessitates a blend of automated tools and manual processes. Automation is pivotal in achieving the speed and consistency required in modern development cycles. However, manual testing remains indispensable for uncovering complex vulnerabilities that automated tools might miss.

Automated Security Testing Tools

1. **Static Application Security Testing (SAST):** SAST tools analyze source code or binaries for vulnerabilities without executing the program. These tools integrate early in the development process, allowing developers to identify and rectify security flaws before code commits. Examples include SonarQube, Checkmarx, and Veracode.

2. **Dynamic Application Security Testing (DAST):** DAST tools test running applications to identify security vulnerabilities that could be exploited in a live environment. These tools simulate external attacks on the application, providing insights into runtime vulnerabilities. Tools like OWASP ZAP and Burp Suite are commonly used.

3. **Interactive Application Security Testing (IAST):** IAST tools combine elements of both SAST and DAST. By monitoring applications in real-time during normal operations or testing phases, IAST provides context-aware vulnerability insights. Examples include Contrast Security and Seeker by Synopsys.

4. **Software Composition Analysis (SCA):** SCA tools examine third-party and open-source components used within the application. Given the prevalence of vulnerabilities in dependencies, SCA tools such as WhiteSource, Black Duck, and Snyk help maintain secure software supply chains.

Manual Security Testing Techniques

1. **Penetration Testing:** Skilled testers simulate real-world attacks to identify vulnerabilities. This method goes beyond automated testing, uncovering logical flaws and complex attack vectors. Regular penetration testing, combined with automated scans, ensures robust security.

2. **Threat Modeling:** This proactive approach involves identifying potential threats and vulnerabilities early in the design phase. By understanding how an attacker

might target the system, developers can design more secure applications from the outset.

3. **Code Review:** Manual code reviews complement automated SAST by providing human insights into potential security issues. Experienced developers and security experts can spot subtle vulnerabilities that automated tools might overlook.

Implementing Security Testing in DevSecOps Pipelines

To effectively integrate security testing into DevSecOps, organizations must re-engineer their CI/CD pipelines to incorporate various security checks at different stages of the SDLC.

Pre-Commit Security Checks

Before developers commit code to the repository, pre-commit hooks can enforce security standards. Automated SAST tools can run quick scans on modified code, ensuring that obvious security flaws are caught early. Additionally, linters and formatters can enforce coding standards that mitigate security risks.

Continuous Integration (CI) Phase

During the CI phase, comprehensive SAST and SCA scans are essential. As code is integrated into the main branch, these tools perform in-depth analyses, providing feedback to developers on potential vulnerabilities. Integration with ticketing systems allows for efficient tracking and remediation of security issues.

Continuous Deployment (CD) Phase

In the CD phase, DAST tools play a critical role. As applications move from staging to production, DAST scans identify vulnerabilities in the deployed environment. Automated testing frameworks can simulate attacks and report findings in real-time, ensuring that only secure code is deployed.

Post-Deployment Monitoring

Security testing does not end at deployment. Continuous monitoring of the production environment is vital to detect and respond to emerging threats. Tools like runtime application self-protection (RASP) and security information and event management (SIEM) systems provide real-time visibility into security incidents.

Challenges and Best Practices

Implementing advanced security testing in a DevSecOps context presents several challenges, including tool integration, performance impacts, and maintaining developer productivity. Addressing these challenges requires a balanced approach and adherence to best practices.

Seamless Tool Integration

Integrating security tools into existing CI/CD pipelines can be complex. Ensuring compatibility and seamless communication between tools is crucial. Utilizing APIs and plugins provided by security tools facilitates smooth integration. Continuous feedback loops between tools and developers ensure that security is embedded without hindering the development process.

Managing Performance Impacts

Security scans, especially comprehensive ones, can introduce latency into the CI/CD pipeline. To mitigate this, organizations can prioritize high-risk components for detailed scans and use incremental scanning techniques that focus on code changes. Parallelizing security tests with other quality assurance activities also helps maintain pipeline efficiency.

Developer Training and Engagement

Developers play a pivotal role in the success of DevSecOps. Providing ongoing security training helps developers understand common vulnerabilities and secure coding practices. Incorporating gamified elements, such as capture-the-flag (CTF) challenges, can make security training engaging and practical.

Culture of Collaboration

A DevSecOps culture promotes collaboration between development, security, and operations teams. Regular cross-functional meetings and shared responsibilities for security foster a sense of ownership and collective accountability. Encouraging open communication and feedback loops ensures that security considerations are part of everyday development practices.

Emerging Trends and Future Directions

As DevSecOps matures, several emerging trends are shaping the future of security testing.

Shift-Left Security

The concept of shift-left security emphasizes addressing security issues as early as possible in the SDLC. This trend encourages developers to adopt secure coding practices and use security tools from the initial stages of development. Shift-left security reduces the cost and complexity of fixing vulnerabilities.

Artificial Intelligence and Machine Learning

AI and ML are revolutionizing security testing by automating the identification of complex attack patterns and vulnerabilities. These technologies enable predictive security analytics, allowing organizations to anticipate and mitigate threats proactively. AI-driven security tools can adapt to evolving threat landscapes, providing more effective protection.

DevSecOps as Code

The rise of "as code" paradigms, such as infrastructure as code (IaC) and policy as code, is extending to security. Security as code involves defining security policies and controls in code, enabling versioning, automated testing, and consistency across environments. This approach streamlines the implementation of security best practices.

Zero Trust Architecture

Zero trust architecture is gaining traction as a security model that assumes no implicit trust within a network. In a DevSecOps context, zero trust principles ensure that every component, whether internal or external, is continuously verified and authenticated. Implementing zero trust enhances the security posture of applications and infrastructure.

Advanced security testing in DevSecOps is essential for developing resilient, secure software in an era where cyber threats are ever-present. By embedding security into every phase of the SDLC and leveraging a combination of automated tools and manual techniques, organizations can effectively identify and mitigate vulnerabilities. Overcoming the challenges of tool integration, performance impacts, and fostering a collaborative culture requires a strategic approach and commitment to continuous improvement. As new technologies and methodologies emerge, staying abreast of these developments ensures that security remains an integral part of the software development process.

Chapter Eight

Advanced Test Reporting and Metrics

Test Metrics for Decision Making

In software development, making informed decisions relies on having accurate and detailed information. Advanced test reporting and metrics provide this crucial information, allowing stakeholders to evaluate the quality, progress, and health of a software project. This text explores the complexities of advanced test reporting and the essential metrics that support decision-making processes.

The Importance of Test Metrics

Test metrics are the quantitative foundation of software quality assurance (QA). They offer insights into various aspects of the testing process, from defect detection rates to test coverage. By systematically analyzing these metrics, QA engineers and project managers can identify trends, pinpoint bottlenecks, and make informed decisions to optimize the development process.

Key Test Metrics for Decision Making

1. Defect Density

Defect density measures the number of defects relative to the size of the software component, often expressed as defects per thousand lines of code (KLOC). This metric helps identify areas of the software that are particularly prone to defects, guiding targeted testing efforts and resource allocation.

By monitoring defect density, teams can assess the quality of different modules and prioritize testing and debugging efforts accordingly.

2. Test Coverage

Test coverage quantifies the extent to which the software is tested. It is typically expressed as a percentage of the total lines of code or functional paths that have been executed by the test suite. High test coverage is indicative of a thorough testing process, reducing the likelihood of undetected defects.

Comprehensive test coverage ensures that all critical paths and edge cases are evaluated, enhancing the overall robustness of the software.

3. Defect Removal Efficiency (DRE)

DRE measures the effectiveness of the testing process in identifying and removing defects before the software is released. It compares the number of defects found and fixed during testing to the total number of defects identified post-release.

High DRE values indicate an efficient testing process, with most defects being caught and addressed before reaching the end users.

4. Mean Time to Detect (MTTD) and Mean Time to Repair (MTTR)

MTTD and MTTR are critical metrics for understanding the responsiveness and effectiveness of the QA team. MTTD measures the average time taken to detect a defect after it is introduced, while MTTR measures the average time taken to fix a defect once it has been identified.

Lower MTTD and MTTR values indicate a proactive and efficient QA process, reducing the impact of defects on the development timeline and product quality.

5. Test Case Effectiveness

Test case effectiveness evaluates the ability of test cases to detect defects. This metric is calculated by dividing the number of defects found by the number of test cases executed.

By analyzing test case effectiveness, QA teams can refine their test suites, focusing on test cases that yield the highest defect detection rates.

6. Requirement Coverage

Requirement coverage assesses the extent to which the software requirements are tested by the test cases. It ensures that all specified requirements are verified, reducing the risk of missing critical functionality.

High requirement coverage signifies that the testing process aligns closely with the project's requirements, ensuring that the final product meets its intended specifications.

Advanced Test Reporting Techniques

Effective test reporting goes beyond the mere presentation of metrics. It involves contextualizing data to provide actionable insights. Here are some advanced test reporting techniques that enhance decision-making:

1. Trend Analysis

Trend analysis involves tracking key metrics over time to identify patterns and trends. By visualizing how metrics such as defect density, test coverage, and DRE evolve, stakeholders can detect early signs of potential issues and take preemptive actions.

2. Root Cause Analysis

Root cause analysis helps identify the underlying causes of defects. By categorizing defects based on their origins, such as requirements, design, coding, or testing, teams can implement targeted improvements to prevent similar issues in the future.

3. Risk-Based Reporting

Risk-based reporting focuses on high-risk areas of the software. By prioritizing metrics and reports that highlight the most critical components, QA teams can allocate resources more effectively, addressing the areas that pose the greatest risk to the project's success.

4. Custom Dashboards

Custom dashboards provide real-time access to key metrics and reports. These dashboards can be tailored to the needs of different stakeholders, offering a quick and intuitive overview of the project's health and progress.

5. Automated Reporting

Automated reporting leverages tools and scripts to generate reports automatically. This approach reduces the manual effort required for report generation, ensuring that stakeholders have timely access to the latest data.

Leveraging Metrics for Decision Making

To maximize the value of test metrics, they must be leveraged effectively in decision-making processes. Here are some best practices for integrating metrics into decision making:

1. Align Metrics with Objectives

Metrics should be aligned with the project's objectives and goals. By focusing on metrics that directly impact project success, teams can ensure that their efforts are aligned with the overall vision.

2. Foster a Data-Driven Culture

Encouraging a data-driven culture within the organization helps integrate metrics into everyday decision-making processes. Regularly reviewing metrics and incorporating them into meetings and discussions ensures that decisions are based on empirical evidence.

3. Balance Quantitative and Qualitative Insights

While metrics provide valuable quantitative data, they should be complemented with qualitative insights from team members. Combining quantitative and qualitative data offers a holistic view of the project's status and potential issues.

4. Use Metrics to Drive Continuous Improvement

Metrics should not only inform decisions but also drive continuous improvement. By regularly reviewing and refining metrics, teams can identify areas for improvement and implement changes that enhance the testing process.

5. Communicate Effectively

Effective communication of metrics is crucial for informed decision-making. Reports should be clear, concise, and tailored to the audience's needs. Visualizations, such as charts and graphs, can help convey complex data in an easily understandable format.

Advanced test reporting and metrics are indispensable tools for software QA engineers. They provide the data needed to assess the quality and progress of software projects, enabling informed decision-making. By leveraging key metrics such as defect density, test coverage, DRE, MTTD, MTTR, test case effectiveness, and requirement coverage, teams can optimize their testing processes and ensure the delivery of high-quality software. Coupled with advanced reporting techniques and best practices for decision-making, these metrics empower QA teams to navigate the complexities of software development with confidence and precision.

Customizing Test Reports

In software quality assurance, generating insightful and actionable test reports is pivotal. These reports are not merely documents; they are critical tools for stakeholders to understand the quality of the software product, the efficiency of the testing process, and areas that need improvement. Customizing these reports to fit the specific needs of a project or organization can significantly enhance their utility. This chapter delves into advanced techniques for tailoring test reports and leveraging metrics to provide maximum value.

Importance of Custom Test Reports

Standard test reports, while useful, often lack the flexibility to cater to the unique requirements of different projects. Each software project has its own set of objectives, risks, and stakeholder expectations. Customizing test reports allows for a more focused and relevant presentation of information, which can aid in better decision-making.

Custom test reports can highlight specific metrics that are most important to the project at hand. For instance, a project with a high emphasis on performance might need detailed performance testing metrics, while another project might prioritize security testing results. By customizing reports, QA engineers can ensure that the most pertinent information is readily available to stakeholders.

Key Components of Test Reports

To effectively customize test reports, it is essential to understand the key components that should be included:

1. **Executive Summary**: A brief overview of the testing activities, highlighting key findings, risks, and recommendations. This section should be concise and written in a non-technical language to be accessible to all stakeholders.

2. **Test Objectives and Scope**: Clearly define the objectives of the testing activities and the scope covered. This helps in setting the context and understanding the focus areas of the testing effort.

3. **Test Methodology**: Describe the approach and techniques used during testing. This might include the types of testing performed (e.g., functional, regression, performance), tools used, and any deviations from the planned test strategy.

4. **Test Metrics and Results**: Present detailed metrics and results of the testing activities. This section can be customized to emphasize specific areas such as defect density, test coverage, pass/fail rates, and other relevant metrics.

5. **Defect Analysis**: Provide an in-depth analysis of the defects found during testing. This should include the number of defects, their severity, priority, and status, as well as trends and patterns observed.

6. **Risk Assessment and Mitigation**: Identify the risks uncovered during testing and suggest mitigation strategies. This is crucial for stakeholders to understand potential impacts on the project timeline and quality.

7. **Conclusion and Recommendations**: Summarize the overall quality of the software product, key takeaways from the testing activities, and provide actionable recommendations for improvement.

Customizing Test Metrics

Metrics play a vital role in conveying the effectiveness of the testing process and the quality of the software. However, not all metrics are equally important for every project. Customizing metrics involves selecting and focusing on those that align with the project's goals and stakeholder expectations. Here are some strategies for customizing test metrics:

1. **Align Metrics with Business Objectives**: Identify the business goals of the project and select metrics that provide insight into these objectives. For instance, if the primary goal is to improve user experience, metrics related to usability testing and customer satisfaction should be prioritized.

2. **Focus on Key Performance Indicators (KPIs)**: Determine the KPIs that are most relevant to the project. This could include metrics like mean time to detect (MTTD), mean time to repair (MTTR), test case effectiveness, and defect leakage rate. KPIs should be chosen based on their ability to provide actionable insights.

3. **Tailor Metrics to Stakeholder Needs**: Different stakeholders have different information needs. For example, project managers might be more interested in metrics related to project timelines and resource

utilization, while developers might focus on defect-related metrics. Customize the report to address these varying needs.

4. **Utilize Visualization Tools**: Visual representations of data can significantly enhance the clarity and impact of test reports. Utilize charts, graphs, and dashboards to present metrics in a more accessible and understandable manner. Tools like Tableau, Power BI, or even Excel can be used to create dynamic and interactive visualizations.

5. **Regularly Review and Update Metrics**: The relevance of certain metrics may change over the course of a project. Regularly review the metrics being tracked and update them as needed to ensure they remain aligned with project goals and stakeholder needs.

Techniques for Effective Customization

Customizing test reports involves more than just selecting the right metrics; it also requires effective presentation and communication of the data. Here are some techniques to achieve this:

1. **Stakeholder Consultation**: Engage with stakeholders early in the project to understand their expectations and information needs. Regular feedback loops can help ensure that the reports remain relevant and useful throughout the project lifecycle.

2. **Modular Reporting**: Design test reports in a modular fashion, where different sections can be easily added, removed, or modified. This allows for greater flexibility

in customization and ensures that the report can be tailored to different audiences without significant rework.

3. **Automated Reporting Tools**: Utilize automated reporting tools that can generate customized reports based on predefined templates and metrics. Tools like Jenkins, JIRA, and TestRail can be integrated with testing frameworks to automatically collect data and generate reports, saving time and reducing the risk of manual errors.

4. **Continuous Improvement**: Establish a process for continuously improving test reports. Collect feedback from stakeholders, analyze the effectiveness of the reports, and make iterative improvements. This approach ensures that the reports evolve with the project and continue to meet stakeholder needs.

5. **Clear and Concise Communication**: Ensure that the language used in the reports is clear and concise. Avoid technical jargon where possible, especially in sections intended for non-technical stakeholders. Use bullet points, tables, and charts to convey information more effectively.

Case Study: Customizing Test Reports for a Financial Software Project

To illustrate the application of these principles, consider a case study of a financial software project. The project involves developing a complex trading platform with stringent performance, security, and regulatory compliance requirements.

Initial Consultation and Requirements Gathering: The QA team begins by consulting with key stakeholders, including project managers, developers, security experts, and end-users. They identify that performance, security, and regulatory compliance are the top priorities.

Selection of Metrics: Based on stakeholder input, the QA team selects a set of metrics that include:

- Performance metrics: response time, transaction throughput, and resource utilization.
- Security metrics: number and severity of security vulnerabilities, time to resolve security issues.
- Compliance metrics: adherence to regulatory standards, number of compliance-related defects.

Custom Report Design: The report is designed to include an executive summary for senior management, detailed technical sections for developers, and a compliance section for regulatory experts. Visualizations such as performance trend graphs, security vulnerability heat maps, and compliance checklists are included to enhance clarity.

Automated Reporting: The team uses automated tools to collect data from various testing tools and frameworks. Jenkins is used to automate the execution of performance tests, and the results are automatically fed into the reporting tool. Similarly, security testing results from tools like OWASP ZAP are integrated into the report.

Continuous Improvement: Regular feedback is collected from stakeholders after each reporting cycle. Based on this feedback, the team iterates on the report design, adding new metrics, refining visualizations, and improving the clarity of the language used.

Customizing test reports and metrics is a critical practice in software quality assurance. It ensures that the most relevant and actionable information is presented to stakeholders, facilitating better decision-making and ultimately leading to higher quality software products. By aligning metrics with business objectives, tailoring reports to stakeholder needs, utilizing visualization tools, and adopting a continuous improvement mindset, QA engineers can create test reports that truly add value to their projects.

Dashboarding and Visualization

In software development, the role of a Quality Assurance (QA) engineer has grown significantly. With the increasing complexity of software, test reporting and metrics have become essential components of the development lifecycle. The need for robust, insightful, and real-time reporting mechanisms is more critical than ever. Advanced test reporting, with a focus on dashboarding and visualization, enhances transparency and drives better decision-making processes.

The Importance of Advanced Test Reporting

Advanced test reporting goes beyond tracking the number of passed or failed test cases. It involves collecting, analyzing, and presenting a wide range of data points that collectively provide a comprehensive view of software quality. Key metrics such as defect density, test coverage, test execution trends, and defect discovery rates need to be captured and analyzed to provide actionable insights.

Effective test reporting serves multiple purposes:

1. **Stakeholder Communication**: Provides clear and concise information to stakeholders, enabling informed decision-making.
2. **Process Improvement**: Identifies bottlenecks and areas for improvement within the testing process.
3. **Risk Management**: Highlights potential risks and areas of concern that need attention.
4. **Regulatory Compliance**: Ensures that the software meets required standards and regulations.

The Role of Dashboarding

A dashboard is a visual representation of key metrics and performance indicators. It provides a snapshot of the current state of testing efforts and highlights trends over time. Dashboards are particularly useful for QA engineers and managers who need to monitor progress, identify issues, and communicate status to stakeholders.

Key Features of Effective Dashboards

1. **Real-Time Data**: Dashboards should provide up-to-date information to accurately reflect the current state of testing efforts.
2. **Customizability**: Different stakeholders have different needs. A customizable dashboard allows users to view the metrics most relevant to them.

3. **Clarity and Simplicity**: Visual representations should be straightforward and easy to interpret. Avoid clutter and focus on key metrics.
4. **Drill-Down Capabilities**: Users should be able to explore data in more detail by drilling down into specific areas of interest.

Common Dashboard Elements

- **Test Execution Summary**: Shows the number of test cases executed, passed, failed, and blocked.
- **Defect Summary**: Displays the number of open, closed, and in-progress defects, along with their severity levels.
- **Test Coverage**: Indicates the percentage of requirements or code covered by tests.
- **Trend Analysis**: Provides visual trends over time, such as the rate of defect discovery and resolution.

Visualization Techniques

Visualization is a powerful tool for making complex data understandable and actionable. By transforming raw data into visual formats, QA engineers can communicate findings more effectively and facilitate better decision-making.

Types of Visualizations

1. **Charts and Graphs**: Line charts, bar charts, and pie charts are commonly used to represent data trends, distributions, and comparisons.

2. **Heatmaps**: Highlight areas with higher concentrations of defects or issues, providing a quick visual cue for where attention is needed.
3. **Histograms**: Show the distribution of a particular data set, such as defect severity or test execution times.
4. **Scatter Plots**: Useful for identifying correlations between different variables, such as test execution time and defect density.
5. **Gantt Charts**: Display the timeline of test activities and milestones, helping to track progress against the schedule.

Best Practices for Visualization

- **Consistency**: Use consistent colors, scales, and formats to avoid confusion.
- **Focus on Key Metrics**: Highlight the most important metrics that drive decision-making.
- **Interactive Elements**: Incorporate interactive elements that allow users to filter and explore data.
- **Annotations and Highlights**: Use annotations and highlights to draw attention to critical insights or anomalies.

Implementing Advanced Test Reporting and Visualization

Implementing advanced test reporting and visualization involves several steps, from selecting the right tools to defining the metrics that matter most to your organization.

Step 1: Define Metrics and KPIs

The first step is to define the metrics and Key Performance Indicators (KPIs) that are most relevant to your testing efforts. This involves understanding the goals of your testing process and identifying the data points that will provide meaningful insights. Common metrics include:

- **Defect Density**: Number of defects per unit of code or test cases.
- **Test Coverage**: Percentage of requirements or code covered by tests.
- **Test Execution Rate**: Number of test cases executed over a specific period.
- **Defect Resolution Time**: Average time taken to resolve defects.

Step 2: Select Tools and Technologies

Choose the tools and technologies that will support your reporting and visualization needs. There are many tools available, ranging from standalone reporting tools to integrated solutions within test management platforms. Key considerations when selecting tools include:

- **Integration**: Ensure the tool can integrate with your existing test management and CI/CD systems.
- **Customization**: Look for tools that offer customizable dashboards and reports.
- **Scalability**: Choose a solution that can handle the volume of data your testing efforts will generate.

- **Ease of Use**: The tool should be user-friendly and require minimal training to use effectively.

Step 3: Collect and Analyze Data

Data collection should be automated as much as possible to ensure accuracy and reduce manual effort. Integrate your test management tools with your CI/CD pipeline to capture data in real-time. Once data is collected, analyze it to identify trends, patterns, and anomalies. Use statistical techniques and machine learning algorithms to derive deeper insights from the data.

Step 4: Design and Implement Dashboards

Design your dashboards with the end user in mind. Consider the needs of different stakeholders and create views that cater to their specific requirements. Use a combination of charts, graphs, and other visual elements to present data in an intuitive and engaging manner. Ensure that dashboards are accessible and can be viewed on different devices, including mobile phones and tablets.

Step 5: Communicate Insights

Effective communication is key to the success of any reporting initiative. Use the insights gained from your dashboards and visualizations to inform stakeholders and drive action. Schedule regular review meetings to discuss findings and update stakeholders on progress. Provide detailed reports and presentations as needed to support decision-making processes.

Challenges and Considerations

While advanced test reporting and visualization offer many benefits, there are also challenges and considerations to keep in mind.

Data Quality and Accuracy

The accuracy of your reports and visualizations depends on the quality of the underlying data. Ensure that data collection processes are robust and that data is validated before it is used for reporting. Regularly audit your data to identify and correct any inconsistencies or errors.

Change Management

Introducing new reporting tools and processes can be met with resistance from team members. Invest in training and change management initiatives to help users understand the benefits of the new approach and how to use the tools effectively.

Scalability

As your testing efforts grow, so will the volume of data you need to manage. Ensure that your reporting and visualization solutions can scale to handle increasing amounts of data without compromising performance.

Security and Privacy

Ensure that your reporting tools comply with security and privacy regulations. Protect sensitive data by implementing appropriate access controls and encryption mechanisms.

Advanced test reporting and metrics, through effective dashboarding and visualization, are essential for modern QA practices. They provide valuable insights that drive better decision-making, improve communication with stakeholders, and enhance the overall quality of software. By implementing robust reporting solutions and following best practices, QA engineers can ensure that they are well-equipped to meet the challenges of today's complex software development environments.

Test Data Analysis Techniques

In today's fast-paced software development environment, advanced test reporting and metrics are crucial for delivering high-quality products. As software projects grow in complexity, the need for comprehensive test data analysis techniques becomes even more evident. This section delves into the essential aspects of advanced test reporting and metrics, focusing on test data analysis techniques that can elevate the effectiveness and accuracy of quality assurance efforts.

The Importance of Advanced Test Reporting

Advanced test reporting provides a detailed view of the testing process, offering insights that go beyond basic pass/fail metrics. These reports are indispensable for stakeholders who need to understand the health and progress of a project. Effective test reporting should address several key areas:

1. **Coverage Analysis**: It's vital to ensure that all aspects of the application are tested. Coverage metrics help identify which parts of the codebase are well-tested and

which areas need more attention. This includes code coverage, requirement coverage, and risk coverage.

2. **Defect Analysis**: Advanced reports should provide detailed information on defects, including their severity, priority, and status. This helps in prioritizing fixes and managing resources effectively.

3. **Trend Analysis**: Observing trends over time can highlight recurring issues and long-term improvements. Metrics such as defect density, test pass rate, and test execution time can reveal significant patterns.

4. **Resource Utilization**: Efficient use of resources, including time and manpower, is critical. Reports should detail how resources are being utilized and suggest areas for improvement.

Key Metrics in Test Reporting

Several metrics are fundamental to advanced test reporting. Understanding and utilizing these metrics can significantly improve the quality of the testing process.

1. **Test Case Effectiveness**: This metric measures the ability of test cases to detect defects. It is calculated by dividing the number of defects found by the number of test cases executed. High effectiveness indicates robust test cases.

2. **Defect Density**: This is the number of defects per unit size of the software, such as lines of code (LOC), function points, or requirements. It helps in identifying high-risk areas that may need more rigorous testing.

3. **Test Execution Rate**: This metric tracks the speed at which test cases are executed. It can be expressed in terms of test cases executed per hour or day and is crucial for measuring the efficiency of the testing process.

4. **Mean Time to Detect (MTTD)**: The average time taken to identify a defect after its introduction into the software. Lower MTTD indicates a more responsive and effective testing process.

5. **Mean Time to Repair (MTTR)**: The average time required to fix a defect once it has been identified. Lower MTTR points to a more efficient development and testing cycle.

Techniques for Test Data Analysis

Test data analysis involves examining the data generated during testing to extract meaningful insights. Advanced techniques can enhance the depth and accuracy of this analysis.

1. **Statistical Analysis**: Utilizing statistical methods to analyze test data can uncover trends and patterns that are not immediately obvious. Techniques such as regression analysis, hypothesis testing, and statistical process control (SPC) can be applied to test metrics to predict future performance and identify potential issues.

2. **Root Cause Analysis (RCA)**: RCA is used to identify the underlying reasons for defects. By systematically investigating the cause of each defect, testers can

develop strategies to prevent similar issues in the future. Common techniques include the 5 Whys, Ishikawa (fishbone) diagrams, and fault tree analysis.

3. **Predictive Analytics**: Leveraging machine learning and artificial intelligence, predictive analytics can forecast potential defects and areas of concern based on historical data. This proactive approach can significantly reduce the occurrence of critical defects in production.

4. **Correlation and Causal Analysis**: Understanding the relationships between different metrics can provide deeper insights into the testing process. For example, correlating defect density with code complexity can reveal whether more complex code areas require additional testing.

5. **Visualization Techniques**: Effective visualization of test data can make complex information more accessible and understandable. Tools like heat maps, trend charts, and scatter plots can highlight key insights and facilitate better decision-making.

Implementing Advanced Test Reporting and Metrics

To implement advanced test reporting and metrics effectively, a structured approach is necessary. Here are some steps to guide the process:

1. **Define Objectives**: Clearly outline the goals of test reporting and the specific metrics that will be used to measure success. Objectives should align with overall project goals and stakeholder needs.

2. **Select Appropriate Tools**: Choose tools that can collect, process, and report on the necessary metrics. Tools should integrate seamlessly with existing development and testing environments.

3. **Data Collection**: Establish a robust process for collecting accurate and comprehensive test data. This includes automating data collection where possible to reduce manual effort and minimize errors.

4. **Data Analysis**: Apply advanced analysis techniques to the collected data. This step involves using statistical methods, machine learning algorithms, and visualization tools to extract actionable insights.

5. **Reporting**: Create detailed and meaningful reports that communicate the findings effectively. Reports should be tailored to the audience, providing high-level overviews for executives and detailed analysis for technical teams.

6. **Review and Improve**: Continuously review the test reporting process and metrics. Solicit feedback from stakeholders and make necessary adjustments to improve the effectiveness of the reports.

Challenges and Considerations

While advanced test reporting and metrics can significantly enhance the quality assurance process, there are several challenges to be aware of:

1. **Data Quality**: The accuracy and completeness of test data are critical. Inaccurate or incomplete data can lead

to misleading conclusions. Implementing rigorous data validation processes can help mitigate this risk.

2. **Tool Integration**: Integrating new tools with existing systems can be complex and time-consuming. Careful planning and testing are essential to ensure a smooth integration.

3. **Resource Constraints**: Advanced test reporting and metrics require significant resources, including time, manpower, and expertise. Balancing these demands with other project requirements can be challenging.

4. **Stakeholder Buy-In**: Gaining support from all stakeholders is crucial for the success of advanced test reporting initiatives. Clear communication of the benefits and involving stakeholders in the process can help achieve buy-in.

Advanced test reporting and metrics are vital components of a comprehensive quality assurance strategy. By leveraging sophisticated test data analysis techniques, organizations can gain deeper insights into their testing processes, identify and mitigate risks, and ultimately deliver higher-quality software products. The implementation of these advanced techniques requires careful planning, appropriate tools, and ongoing review, but the benefits far outweigh the challenges. By focusing on the key metrics and analysis techniques outlined in this section, software QA engineers can elevate their testing processes and contribute significantly to the success of their projects.

Chapter Nine

Test Automation Infrastructure

Test Environment Setup

In the realm of software quality assurance (QA), the establishment of a robust test automation infrastructure is crucial for ensuring the reliability and efficiency of software products. This infrastructure serves as the backbone, facilitating the seamless execution of automated tests across various environments. This article delves into the essential components and methodologies involved in setting up a cohesive test environment, emphasizing the importance of meticulous planning and systematic implementation.

Understanding Test Automation Infrastructure

At its core, test automation infrastructure comprises a set of tools, frameworks, and resources designed to support the automated testing process. Its primary objective is to simulate real-world scenarios and validate software functionalities under controlled conditions. A well-structured infrastructure not only accelerates testing cycles but also enhances test coverage and accuracy.

Key Components of Test Automation Infrastructure

1. **Test Environment Configuration**: Setting up a conducive test environment begins with identifying the

hardware and software prerequisites necessary for testing. This involves configuring servers, databases, networks, and other dependencies to mirror production environments accurately. Virtualization technologies such as Docker and virtual machines play a crucial role in achieving environment consistency and scalability.

2. **Test Automation Frameworks**: Selecting an appropriate automation framework is pivotal in defining the testing approach. Frameworks like Selenium, Appium, and JUnit provide the necessary tools and libraries to create and execute automated test scripts effectively. Framework choice depends on factors such as application type, scalability requirements, and team proficiency.

3. **Version Control Systems (VCS)**: Implementing a robust VCS such as Git ensures version management and collaboration among team members. VCS enables seamless integration of automated tests with continuous integration/continuous deployment (CI/CD) pipelines, facilitating automated execution triggered by code changes.

4. **CI/CD Integration**: Integrating test automation into CI/CD pipelines accelerates the feedback loop and promotes early bug detection. Tools like Jenkins, Travis CI, or GitLab CI automate the build, test, and deployment processes, enabling teams to achieve faster time-to-market without compromising quality.

5. **Configuration Management**: Tools such as Ansible, Puppet, or Chef automate the provisioning and configuration of test environments. They ensure

consistency across different environments and streamline the setup of infrastructure components required for testing.

6. **Test Data Management**: Managing test data effectively is crucial for executing comprehensive test scenarios. Tools like Test Data Management (TDM) solutions or database seeding scripts facilitate the creation, manipulation, and cleanup of test data, ensuring test repeatability and reliability.

Best Practices for Test Environment Setup

1. **Infrastructure as Code (IaC)**: Embracing IaC principles using tools like Terraform or CloudFormation automates the provisioning and configuration of infrastructure components. This approach enhances environment reproducibility, scalability, and reduces manual errors.

2. **Environment Isolation**: Maintaining isolated testing environments minimizes interference between tests and ensures accurate results. Techniques such as containerization or virtualization help achieve environment isolation while optimizing resource utilization.

3. **Continuous Monitoring**: Implementing monitoring tools like Prometheus or Nagios provides real-time insights into environment health and test execution status. Proactive monitoring detects anomalies early, ensuring timely intervention and minimizing downtime.

4. **Security Considerations**: Securing test environments with access controls, encryption, and vulnerability assessments safeguards sensitive data and prevents unauthorized access. Incorporating security testing into automated pipelines ensures software resilience against potential threats.

Challenges and Considerations

Despite its benefits, establishing a robust test automation infrastructure entails overcoming several challenges:

- **Complexity**: Managing diverse technologies and integrations requires expertise in multiple areas, from testing and infrastructure to automation and DevOps.

- **Maintenance**: Regular updates, patches, and configuration changes necessitate proactive maintenance to sustain infrastructure reliability and performance.

- **Cost**: Investing in tools, resources, and skilled personnel for infrastructure setup and maintenance can incur substantial costs.

In conclusion, building a resilient test automation infrastructure involves meticulous planning, leveraging suitable tools, and adhering to best practices. A well-structured setup not only enhances testing efficiency but also accelerates software delivery while maintaining high standards of quality. By embracing automation, continuous integration, and scalable infrastructure, organizations can streamline their testing processes and achieve greater agility in today's competitive software development environment.

I Infrastructure as Code (IaC)

Crafting a robust Test Automation Infrastructure (TAI) through Infrastructure as Code (IaC) is crucial for contemporary software QA engineers aiming to streamline testing processes and enhance product reliability. TAI serves as the foundational framework supporting automated testing across diverse software environments, ensuring efficiency, scalability, and consistency in testing practices.

TAI leverages IaC principles to automate the provisioning, configuration, and management of essential infrastructure components for testing. Unlike traditional manual setups prone to human error and inconsistency, TAI using IaC allows engineers to programmatically define infrastructure requirements. This approach treats infrastructure akin to software, enabling version-controlled, tested, and deployable infrastructure alongside application code. This promotes agility and reproducibility in testing environments.

Key Components of Test Automation Infrastructure

1. Infrastructure Provisioning

TAI begins with provisioning infrastructure resources such as virtual machines, containers, networks, and storage. Tools like Terraform or AWS CloudFormation enable engineers to specify infrastructure state through declarative configuration files. These files define parameters such as server specifications, networking rules, and storage requirements, ensuring consistent environment provisioning across development, testing, and production stages.

2. Configuration Management

Post-provisioning, configuring infrastructure components is crucial to ensure compatibility with testing frameworks and applications. Configuration management tools like Ansible or Chef automate the setup and deployment of necessary software packages, libraries, and dependencies for testing. This ensures correctly configured testing environments, reducing setup time and eliminating configuration discrepancies that could impact testing consistency.

3. Continuous Integration and Deployment (CI/CD)

Integrating TAI into CI/CD pipelines is essential for achieving rapid feedback and continuous testing. CI/CD pipelines automate the build, test, and deployment of software applications and associated testing environments. By incorporating TAI into CI/CD workflows using tools like Jenkins or GitLab CI/CD, teams automate test suite execution against various application versions. This ensures thorough validation of changes before deployment, promoting software quality and reliability.

4. Monitoring and Reporting

Effective monitoring and reporting are integral to TAI, offering insights into test execution, infrastructure performance, and test coverage. Monitoring tools such as Prometheus or ELK stack provide real-time monitoring of infrastructure metrics and application logs. This enables proactive issue identification and resolution, ensuring testing outcomes remain robust. Detailed test reports generated through tools like JUnit or Allure provide stakeholders with actionable insights into test results, facilitating informed decision-making and continuous testing process improvement.

Benefits of Test Automation Infrastructure

1. Enhanced Efficiency and Consistency

TAI automates repetitive tasks involved in provisioning and managing testing environments, reducing manual effort and minimizing errors. By ensuring consistent infrastructure configuration across environments, TAI promotes reliable and reproducible testing outcomes, enhancing testing efficiency.

2. Scalability and Flexibility

IaC enables TAI to scale seamlessly to meet varying testing requirements and workload fluctuations. Engineers can dynamically provision and decommission testing environments based on demand, optimizing resource utilization and reducing costs associated with idle resources.

3. Accelerated Time-to-Market

Automating infrastructure setup and configuration accelerates the testing process, enabling faster delivery of software updates and new features to end-users. Rapid feedback cycles facilitated by CI/CD integration ensure quality issues are identified early in the development lifecycle, minimizing time spent on bug fixes and rework.

4. Improved Collaboration and Transparency

TAI fosters collaboration between development, QA, and operations teams by providing a shared understanding of infrastructure requirements and configurations. Version-controlled infrastructure code enhances transparency and accountability, allowing teams to track changes, review history, and collaborate effectively on infrastructure improvements.

Challenges and Considerations

While TAI offers numerous benefits, its implementation requires addressing several challenges:

- **Complexity:** Managing complex infrastructure configurations and dependencies using IaC tools demands expertise in scripting and automation.
- **Security:** Ensuring the security of automated infrastructure deployments and managing access controls to sensitive resources is critical to preventing vulnerabilities and unauthorized access.
- **Tool Selection:** Selecting the right combination of IaC and automation tools tailored to project requirements and infrastructure environments is essential for maximizing the effectiveness of TAI.

In conclusion, Test Automation Infrastructure powered by Infrastructure as Code represents a fundamental shift in how software QA engineers approach testing. By automating infrastructure provisioning, configuration, and management, TAI enhances testing efficiency, scalability, and reliability, thereby accelerating time-to-market and improving software quality. Embracing TAI not only streamlines testing processes but also fosters collaboration, transparency, and innovation across development and operations teams, facilitating continuous improvement and delivery of high-quality software products.

Containerization and Orchestration

In the dynamic landscape of software development, ensuring the quality and reliability of applications through robust testing practices is crucial. Among the key advancements in this area is the adoption of containerization and orchestration technologies within test automation infrastructure. This integration not only simplifies the deployment and management of testing environments but also enhances the efficiency and scalability of automated testing processes.

Containerization: Enhancing Portability and Consistency

Containerization is a transformative approach to software deployment, encapsulating applications and their dependencies into portable units known as containers. By leveraging the isolation capabilities of the operating system, containers allow applications to run consistently across different computing environments. For test automation, containers offer several advantages.

Firstly, containers ensure consistency across development, testing, and production environments. By packaging the entire testing setup—including libraries, dependencies, and configurations—into a single, self-contained unit, containerization reduces compatibility issues that often affect traditional testing setups. This consistency minimizes discrepancies between testing phases, enhancing the reliability of test results and the accuracy of quality assessments.

Moreover, containerization facilitates seamless integration with continuous integration and continuous deployment (CI/CD) pipelines, which are essential for modern software delivery practices. By enabling developers to package tests alongside their dependencies, containers speed up the deployment of testing environments. This agility accelerates time-to-market and fosters a culture of iterative improvement within development cycles.

Furthermore, containers promote scalability by using lightweight virtualization technology. Test automation frameworks can deploy multiple instances of testing environments simultaneously, allowing teams to conduct concurrent testing across various configurations and scenarios. This scalability is particularly beneficial in distributed development environments or complex application architectures where simulating diverse usage conditions is critical for comprehensive testing coverage.

Orchestration: Streamlining Management and Optimization

While containerization focuses on deploying and encapsulating testing environments, orchestration plays a crucial role in automating and managing these containerized resources on a larger scale. Orchestration frameworks like Kubernetes have become essential for coordinating containerized workloads, providing functionalities for deployment, scaling, and resource allocation in distributed computing environments.

At its core, orchestration simplifies the complexities of managing containerized applications across multiple nodes. By abstracting the underlying infrastructure and providing a unified control plane, orchestration frameworks enable teams to focus on defining and executing test scenarios rather than managing resource provisioning.

Additionally, orchestration enhances the resilience and fault tolerance of test automation infrastructure. Automated health checks, load balancing, and self-healing mechanisms ensure that testing workloads continue to operate reliably even during node failures or unexpected increases in demand. This resilience is crucial for maintaining testing operations and preserving the integrity of test results in dynamic development environments.

Furthermore, orchestration promotes collaboration and efficiency within cross-functional teams by integrating testing processes seamlessly into broader CI/CD workflows. By standardizing deployment practices and promoting consistent testing methodologies across different stages of the software development lifecycle, orchestration frameworks enable organizations to achieve greater agility and alignment in their quality assurance practices.

Future Directions and Considerations

Looking forward, the convergence of containerization and orchestration technologies is set to drive further innovations in test automation infrastructure. As organizations increasingly adopt DevOps principles and strive for greater automation and efficiency, integrating these technologies will play a pivotal role in shaping the future of software testing.

However, while containerization and orchestration offer significant benefits, their adoption requires careful consideration of several factors. Organizations must assess the scalability needs of their testing infrastructure, evaluate the compatibility of existing tools and frameworks with containerized environments, and invest in training to equip teams with the necessary expertise.

In conclusion, the integration of containerization and orchestration technologies represents a fundamental shift in test automation infrastructure. By enhancing portability, consistency, scalability, and manageability of testing environments, these technologies empower organizations to accelerate software delivery cycles, improve product quality, and meet the demands of today's dynamic market environments.

Cloud-Based Test Automation

In today's software development scene, the integration of cloud computing has brought significant changes, particularly in software testing. A notable advancement is the adoption of cloud-based test automation infrastructure. This approach not only boosts scalability and flexibility but also enhances the efficiency of software quality assurance (QA) processes.

The Shift to Cloud-Based Test Automation

Traditionally, software QA teams relied on on-site infrastructure for test automation. While effective, this setup often struggled with scalability and resource management issues. As applications became more complex and user bases expanded globally, the need for more robust and scalable testing solutions became evident.

The advent of cloud computing fundamentally transformed IT infrastructure. Cloud platforms offered scalability, on-demand resource allocation, and geographic distribution capabilities. Recognizing these benefits, organizations quickly began moving their software development and testing environments to the cloud.

Benefits of Cloud-Based Test Automation Infrastructure

Cloud-based test automation infrastructure offers several advantages over traditional setups. One key benefit is scalability. Cloud platforms allow QA teams to scale their testing efforts dynamically based on project needs and user demands. This flexibility ensures optimal utilization of testing resources without the inefficiencies of over-provisioning or underutilization.

Additionally, cloud-based infrastructure improves flexibility in testing environments. QA engineers can easily set up various testing environments to accommodate different configurations, operating systems, and network conditions. This capability is crucial for testing applications intended for global deployment, ensuring robust performance and reliability across diverse user scenarios.

Cost efficiency is another compelling advantage of cloud-based test automation infrastructure. By leveraging cloud services, organizations eliminate the need for large upfront investments in hardware and infrastructure maintenance. Instead, they adopt a pay-as-you-go model where costs align with actual usage. This not only reduces capital expenditures but also optimizes operational expenses related to maintaining and upgrading on-premises hardware.

Technical Considerations and Implementation

Implementing cloud-based test automation infrastructure requires careful planning and consideration of various technical aspects. A fundamental component of this infrastructure is the use of virtualization and containerization technologies. Virtual machines (VMs) and containers encapsulate testing environments, ensuring consistency and reproducibility across different stages of the software development lifecycle (SDLC).

Furthermore, cloud providers offer a range of managed services tailored for testing and QA purposes. These services include scalable test execution environments, integrated continuous integration and delivery (CI/CD) pipelines, and comprehensive monitoring and analytics tools. Such services enable QA teams to automate test workflows, detect defects early in the development cycle, and expedite the delivery of high-quality software products.

Security and compliance are critical concerns when adopting cloud-based test automation infrastructure. Cloud providers adhere to strict security standards and certifications, ensuring data protection and regulatory compliance across different regions. QA engineers must implement robust access controls, encryption methods, and vulnerability management practices to safeguard sensitive testing data and intellectual property.

Best Practices and Challenges

Successful implementation of cloud-based test automation infrastructure requires adherence to best practices and proactive management of challenges. Establishing clear governance policies, including resource allocation, usage monitoring, and cost management, is essential for optimizing cloud expenditure and maintaining budgetary discipline.

Additionally, QA teams must continuously evaluate and leverage emerging technologies and tools within the cloud ecosystem. Techniques such as serverless computing, AI-driven testing automation, and machine learning-based anomaly detection offer innovative opportunities to enhance test coverage, improve defect detection rates, and streamline QA workflows.

Despite its numerous benefits, adopting cloud-based test automation infrastructure presents inherent challenges. These challenges include managing vendor lock-in risks, ensuring compatibility with legacy systems, and mitigating potential performance bottlenecks associated with cloud service outages or latency issues. Proactive risk management and contingency planning are essential to mitigate these challenges and ensure uninterrupted testing operations.

Future Trends and Innovations

Looking ahead, the evolution of cloud-based test automation infrastructure will be influenced by emerging trends and technological advancements. One significant trend is the convergence of DevOps and AI-driven automation, where AI algorithms analyze extensive testing data to predict potential defects and optimize test case selection dynamically.

Furthermore, the rise of hybrid and multi-cloud environments is expected to redefine the scalability and resilience of test automation infrastructure. Organizations will increasingly adopt hybrid cloud architectures to distribute workloads across multiple cloud providers, enhancing redundancy and reducing risks associated with single-point-of-failure.

In conclusion, cloud-based test automation infrastructure represents a significant shift in software QA practices, offering unparalleled scalability, flexibility, and cost efficiency. By embracing cloud computing, organizations can accelerate time-to-market, enhance software quality, and adapt swiftly to evolving market demands. As technology continues to evolve, the synergy between cloud computing and test automation will drive innovation and excellence in software development and QA disciplines.

Chapter Ten

Advanced CI/CD Practices

CI/CD Pipelines Orchestration

In today's fast-paced software development environment, Continuous Integration and Continuous Delivery (CI/CD) practices have become essential for efficiently delivering high-quality software products. Central to these practices is CI/CD pipeline orchestration, a sophisticated approach that automates and coordinates software development workflows from code integration to deployment.

Understanding CI/CD Pipeline Orchestration

CI/CD pipeline orchestration involves automating key stages of the software development lifecycle (SDLC), including code integration, testing, deployment, and delivery. This orchestration ensures smooth workflow execution, enabling development teams to identify and rectify issues early, speed up release cycles, and maintain consistent software quality throughout development.

Key Components and Workflow Automation

An essential aspect of CI/CD pipeline orchestration is integrating various tools and technologies to automate workflow stages effectively. Typically, CI/CD pipelines consist of interconnected stages:

1. **Source Code Management:** Developers commit code changes to a version control system like Git, initiating the CI/CD pipeline.

2. **Build Automation:** Automated build processes compile source code into executable artifacts, ensuring consistency and reliability across different development environments.

3. **Automated Testing:** Continuous integration involves running automated tests (unit, integration, and acceptance tests) to validate code changes and catch potential issues early in the development cycle.

4. **Deployment Automation:** Continuous delivery automates the deployment of validated code changes to staging or production environments, using infrastructure as code (IaC) principles to maintain environment consistency.

5. **Release Automation:** Automated release processes ensure smooth deployment to end-users, incorporating rollback mechanisms and progressive delivery techniques to minimize downtime and reduce risks.

Benefits of CI/CD Pipeline Orchestration

CI/CD pipeline orchestration offers numerous advantages that enhance the efficiency and reliability of software development and delivery processes. One significant benefit is accelerated time-to-market. By automating repetitive tasks and integrating automated testing, CI/CD pipelines reduce manual intervention, enabling development teams to release new features and updates swiftly and consistently.

Moreover, CI/CD pipeline orchestration promotes collaboration and transparency across development and operations teams. By establishing standardized workflows and automated feedback mechanisms, CI/CD pipelines facilitate continuous improvement and iterative development practices, fostering agility and innovation within organizations.

Technical Considerations and Implementation Challenges

Implementing CI/CD pipeline orchestration requires careful consideration of technical and organizational factors. Technical considerations include selecting suitable CI/CD tools and technologies, configuring pipeline workflows, and seamlessly integrating with existing development and deployment infrastructure.

Organizations must also address implementation challenges such as ensuring pipeline scalability, managing dependencies across interconnected services, and maintaining security and compliance standards throughout the CI/CD process. Effective governance and monitoring mechanisms are crucial to mitigate risks associated with pipeline failures, performance bottlenecks, and infrastructure vulnerabilities.

Best Practices and Continuous Optimization

Successful CI/CD pipeline orchestration relies on adopting best practices and embracing continuous optimization strategies. Organizations should prioritize modular and reusable pipeline components, enabling scalability and flexibility to meet evolving project requirements and technological advancements.

Integrating feedback loops and automated quality gates enhances pipeline reliability and software quality. Proactive monitoring and analytics provide real-time visibility into pipeline performance metrics, facilitating timely identification and resolution of bottlenecks and inefficiencies.

Future Trends and Innovations

Looking ahead, the evolution of CI/CD pipeline orchestration will be shaped by emerging trends and innovations. One notable trend is the integration of AI-driven analytics and machine learning algorithms to automate anomaly detection, optimize pipeline performance, and predict potential issues proactively.

Additionally, the adoption of cloud-native architectures and serverless computing models is expected to redefine the scalability and resilience of CI/CD pipeline infrastructure. Organizations will increasingly leverage microservices-based architectures and container orchestration platforms like Kubernetes to enhance deployment flexibility and resource efficiency.

In conclusion, CI/CD pipeline orchestration is fundamental to modern software development practices, enabling organizations to achieve continuous integration, delivery, and deployment with unprecedented efficiency and reliability. By embracing automation, collaboration, and iterative improvement, organizations can accelerate innovation, deliver value to stakeholders, and maintain a competitive edge in today's dynamic market.

Canary and Blue-Green Deployments

In today's fast-paced software development, Continuous Integration and Continuous Deployment (CI/CD) practices have transformed how software updates are managed and delivered. Among the more sophisticated strategies gaining popularity are Canary and Blue-Green deployments, methods designed to enhance deployment reliability and minimize downtime through incremental updates and parallel environments.

Canary Deployments: Testing the Waters

Canary deployments involve rolling out updates to a small subset, or "canary group," of users or servers before full deployment. This approach acts as an early warning system, allowing teams to closely monitor the new release's performance in a controlled environment. By exposing a fraction of the user base to the update, developers can quickly identify and address potential issues before they affect a larger audience.

Successful Canary deployments rely on thorough planning and monitoring. Automated testing frameworks, combined with real-time telemetry and logging, provide valuable insights into the update's impact. Metrics such as error rates, latency, and user feedback help assess the update's stability and user satisfaction. Continuous monitoring ensures that any anomalies are promptly detected and resolved, safeguarding the overall user experience.

Blue-Green Deployments: Seamless Transitions with Minimal Disruption

In contrast, Blue-Green deployments focus on maintaining uninterrupted service during updates by maintaining two identical production environments: one active (Green) and one inactive (Blue). Updates are first deployed to the inactive environment, allowing ample time for testing and validation. Once verified, traffic is smoothly redirected to the updated environment, minimizing downtime and eliminating the risk of disruptions.

A key advantage of Blue-Green deployments is their ability to facilitate quick rollback in case of unexpected issues. Reverting to the previous environment is swift and seamless, ensuring continuity of service with minimal impact on end-users. This redundancy not only enhances deployment reliability but also instills confidence in the deployment process, fostering a culture of innovation and experimentation within development teams.

Best Practices for Implementation

Implementing Canary and Blue-Green deployments requires a combination of technical expertise and strategic planning. Key considerations include:

1. **Automated Testing and Validation**: Comprehensive test automation frameworks are essential for validating updates across different environments. Automated tests should cover functional, integration, and performance testing to verify both the update's functionality and its impact on system performance.

2. **Gradual Rollouts**: Incremental deployment in Canary deployments allows teams to identify and mitigate issues early, reducing the risk of widespread disruption. Automated rollback mechanisms further bolster resilience by ensuring rapid recovery from deployment failures.

3. **Continuous Monitoring and Feedback**: Real-time monitoring of key performance indicators (KPIs) enables proactive detection of anomalies and performance degradation. User feedback mechanisms, such as A/B testing and feature toggles, facilitate iterative improvements based on user preferences and behavior.

4. **Infrastructure as Code (IaC)**: Embracing Infrastructure as Code principles simplifies environment provisioning and configuration management, ensuring consistent deployments across different environments. Tools like Terraform and Ansible automate infrastructure setup, minimizing deployment overhead and maintaining environment parity in Blue-Green deployments.

5. **Cultural Adoption and Continuous Improvement**: Successful adoption of advanced CI/CD practices hinges on promoting a collaborative culture focused on experimentation and continuous improvement across development teams. Encouraging knowledge sharing and cross-functional collaboration accelerates learning cycles and enhances the effectiveness of deployment strategies over time.

Canary and Blue-Green deployments represent significant advancements in CI/CD practices, offering developers enhanced flexibility and reliability in managing software updates. By leveraging incremental rollout strategies and parallel environments, teams can minimize deployment risks, optimize system performance, and deliver seamless user experiences. Embracing these advanced practices not only enhances deployment reliability but also empowers teams to innovate rapidly and respond to market demands with agility.

In the evolving landscape of software engineering, Canary and Blue-Green deployments demonstrate the transformative impact of continuous improvement and adaptive deployment strategies. As organizations strive for greater efficiency and resilience in software delivery, these methodologies promise to remain essential tools in the modern developer's toolkit.

Automated Rollback Strategies

In the fast-paced world of software development and deployment, Continuous Integration and Continuous Deployment (CI/CD) have become essential methodologies for ensuring rapid and reliable application delivery. Central to these practices is the concept of automated rollback strategies, which play a crucial role in maintaining system stability and minimizing downtime in case of deployment failures or issues.

Understanding Automated Rollback Strategies

Automated rollback strategies are designed to automatically revert a deployment to a previous stable state when issues arise during the deployment process. These issues could range from bugs found in the new release to performance degradation or unexpected errors affecting user experience. By swiftly rolling back to a known stable version, teams can mitigate the impact of such issues and promptly restore service reliability.

Importance of Automated Rollbacks in CI/CD

In CI/CD pipelines, where changes to application code are frequent and automated testing and deployment are standard practices, the ability to rollback efficiently is critical. Traditional rollback methods often involve manual intervention, which can introduce delays and increase the risk of human error. Automated rollback strategies address these challenges by enabling immediate response to deployment failures without needing human intervention.

Key Components of Effective Automated Rollback Strategies

1. Health Checks and Monitoring:

Automated rollback strategies start with comprehensive health checks and monitoring systems. These systems continuously monitor key metrics like system performance, resource usage, and application health indicators. Pre-defined thresholds and deviations in metrics trigger alerts that start the rollback process upon detecting anomalies.

2. Versioning and State Management:

Central to automated rollback strategies is robust versioning and state management. Each deployment version is carefully tracked and tagged to ensure traceability and the ability to revert to a specific stable state when required. Version control systems and configuration management tools play a crucial role in maintaining consistency across environments and facilitating seamless rollback procedures.

3. Automated Testing and Validation:

Before deployment, automated testing frameworks validate the integrity and functionality of the application. These tests include unit tests, integration tests, and end-to-end tests that simulate user interactions. Successful completion of these tests is a prerequisite for deployment, ensuring that only validated changes are pushed to production environments and reducing the likelihood of rollback.

4. Incremental Rollouts and Canary Deployments:

Advanced CI/CD pipelines often use incremental rollout strategies, where changes are gradually deployed to a subset of users or servers. Canary deployments allow teams to monitor the impact of changes in a controlled environment before a full rollout. These practices minimize the scope of potential issues and provide early detection mechanisms that inform decisions regarding rollback actions.

5. Fault Detection and Automated Decision-Making:

Automated rollback strategies incorporate fault detection mechanisms that analyze real-time data and performance metrics. Machine learning algorithms and anomaly detection techniques enhance the system's ability to identify abnormal behavior patterns and initiate automated decisions. This proactive approach reduces the time between issue detection and rollback initiation, thereby minimizing service downtime and enhancing overall reliability.

Implementing Automated Rollback Strategies

Implementing automated rollback strategies requires technical expertise, collaboration across development and operations teams, and adherence to best practices. Key steps include:

- **Defining Rollback Triggers:** Establish clear criteria and thresholds that determine when a rollback should be triggered, based on predefined metrics and performance benchmarks.

- **Automating Deployment Pipelines:** Seamlessly integrate rollback mechanisms into CI/CD pipelines, ensuring that rollback processes are automatically triggered in response to detected failures or anomalies.

- **Testing and Validation:** Conduct rigorous testing of rollback procedures in staging environments to validate their effectiveness and reliability under simulated failure scenarios.

- **Monitoring and Feedback Loops:** Continuously monitor the effectiveness of automated rollback strategies and gather feedback from stakeholders to identify areas for improvement and optimization.

Case Studies and Real-World Applications

Many organizations have successfully implemented automated rollback strategies to enhance their CI/CD workflows and improve deployment reliability. For instance, a leading e-commerce platform uses automated canary deployments combined with automated rollback mechanisms to ensure smooth updates to their online storefront. By leveraging real-time monitoring and automated decision-making, the platform minimizes the impact of potential issues on customer experience and maintains high availability throughout the deployment process.

In conclusion, automated rollback strategies are fundamental to advanced CI/CD practices, providing organizations with the means to maintain agility while ensuring system reliability. By integrating automated rollback mechanisms into CI/CD pipelines and emphasizing proactive monitoring and testing, teams can effectively mitigate risks associated with deployment failures and accelerate the pace of innovation. As software development continues to evolve, the adoption of robust automated rollback strategies will remain essential for achieving continuous delivery and meeting the demands of modern digital environments.

Infrastructure Testing in CI/CD Pipelines

In today's fast-paced software development environment, Continuous Integration and Continuous Delivery (CI/CD) pipelines have become indispensable for ensuring efficient and reliable software delivery. A crucial aspect of these pipelines is infrastructure testing, which focuses on validating the stability and performance of the underlying systems that support applications.

CI/CD pipelines automate various stages of software delivery, including code compilation, testing, and deployment. However, the effectiveness of these pipelines relies heavily on the reliability of the infrastructure—servers, databases, and networking components. Infrastructure testing within CI/CD pipelines addresses this critical need by verifying the infrastructure's scalability, reliability, and performance throughout the software development cycle.

The Role of Infrastructure Testing

Infrastructure testing involves a range of practices aimed at assessing and confirming the performance and reliability of the infrastructure that supports applications. Unlike traditional testing methods that focus primarily on application functionality, infrastructure testing delves into the operational aspects of the software ecosystem.

Types of Infrastructure Testing

1. **Configuration Testing**: Ensures that the configuration of servers, databases, and other infrastructure components aligns with the application's requirements. This includes validating network settings, firewall rules, and load balancer configurations to ensure they support the application's needs without compromising security or performance.

2. **Performance Testing**: Evaluates how well the infrastructure handles various loads and stress levels. Performance testing identifies potential bottlenecks and ensures that the infrastructure can manage expected user traffic without service degradation.

3. **Security Testing**: Identifies vulnerabilities and weaknesses in the infrastructure that could be exploited by malicious actors. This includes conducting penetration testing and vulnerability assessments to ensure compliance with security standards and regulations.

4. **Resilience Testing**: Assesses the infrastructure's ability to recover from failures and disruptions. This involves simulating failures such as server crashes or network outages to validate redundancy measures and disaster recovery plans.

Implementing Infrastructure Testing in CI/CD Pipelines

Integrating infrastructure testing into CI/CD pipelines requires careful planning and execution to ensure seamless automation and timely feedback. Here's how organizations can effectively incorporate these practices:

1. **Automated Testing Suites**: Develop comprehensive automated test suites that cover different aspects of infrastructure performance, security, and resilience. These tests should provide quick feedback on the infrastructure's health.

2. **Continuous Monitoring**: Implement robust monitoring solutions to gain real-time insights into infrastructure performance and availability. Monitoring metrics like CPU usage, memory utilization, and network response times help detect anomalies early and prevent potential issues.

3. **Infrastructure as Code (IaC)**: Embrace Infrastructure as Code principles to manage infrastructure configurations programmatically. Treating infrastructure configurations as code allows for version control, automated testing, and deployment practices similar to those used for application code.

4. **Integration with CI/CD Pipelines**: Incorporate infrastructure testing into key stages of CI/CD pipelines, such as during code commits, build processes, and deployment cycles. Automated tests should trigger automatically when changes are made to infrastructure configurations or application code.

Benefits of Infrastructure Testing in CI/CD Pipelines

Implementing advanced infrastructure testing practices in CI/CD pipelines offers several benefits for organizations:

- **Enhanced Reliability and Stability**: Early detection of infrastructure issues reduces downtime and ensures consistent performance, enhancing overall system reliability.

- **Accelerated Time to Market**: Automated testing and continuous validation speed up the delivery of updates and new features by minimizing deployment failures and rollbacks.

- **Improved Security Posture**: Proactive security testing helps identify and mitigate vulnerabilities before they are exploited, reducing the risk of security breaches and data loss.

- **Cost Efficiency**: By identifying and addressing infrastructure inefficiencies early in the development process, organizations can optimize resource usage and lower operational costs.

In conclusion, infrastructure testing is critical for ensuring the resilience, performance, and security of modern software applications deployed through CI/CD pipelines. By integrating advanced testing practices into development workflows, organizations can mitigate risks, accelerate time to market, and deliver high-quality software solutions. As software development continues to advance, robust infrastructure testing remains a valuable investment for organizations committed to delivering reliable and efficient software solutions.

Chapter Eleven

Advanced Quality Assurance Techniques

Shift-Left Testing

Quality assurance (QA) stands as an essential pillar, ensuring that software products meet high standards of functionality, reliability, and usability. Amid the evolving methodologies and practices, "Shift-Left Testing" emerges as a pivotal strategy, redefining how QA integrates with the development lifecycle.

Traditionally, QA activities were typically performed in the later stages of development, often after implementation. However, with the rise of Agile methodologies and continuous integration, a new approach is necessary. Shift-Left Testing advocates for the early involvement of QA processes right from the beginning of a project, aiming to detect and rectify defects as close to their origin as possible—thus minimizing their impact on subsequent phases.

At its core, Shift-Left Testing embodies proactive rather than reactive QA practices. By involving QA specialists during initial project planning and requirements gathering, teams can identify potential risks and ambiguities early on. This early collaboration fosters a shared understanding among stakeholders, aligning development efforts with quality objectives from the outset.

One of the fundamental principles of Shift-Left Testing is the integration of QA into the continuous integration and continuous delivery (CI/CD) pipeline. By automating tests and leveraging robust version control systems, teams can achieve rapid feedback loops, enabling developers to promptly address issues as they arise. This iterative approach not only speeds up time-to-market but also enhances product stability through consistent validation.

Moreover, Shift-Left Testing promotes a comprehensive test strategy that covers various levels of testing—unit, integration, system, and acceptance testing—throughout the development lifecycle. Each phase serves a distinct purpose, validating both individual components and their collective functionality within the broader system architecture. By conducting thorough tests early on, teams can identify potential bottlenecks and compatibility issues beforehand, fostering a more resilient product ecosystem.

Furthermore, the effectiveness of Shift-Left Testing relies on robust test automation frameworks and tools. Automation not only speeds up repetitive test scenarios but also ensures consistent test coverage across multiple platforms and environments. By reducing manual intervention, teams can allocate resources towards more complex test scenarios and exploratory testing, thereby enhancing overall test depth and accuracy.

In practice, adopting Shift-Left Testing requires a cultural shift within organizations, promoting collaboration and transparency across cross-functional teams. Quality assurance professionals, equipped with domain expertise, play a crucial role in guiding developers towards adopting best practices and quality benchmarks. Through continuous knowledge sharing and skills development, teams can cultivate a culture of quality ownership, where every team member assumes responsibility for delivering high-quality software solutions.

Ultimately, the adoption of Shift-Left Testing represents a strategic investment in mitigating risks and improving the overall quality of software products. By embracing proactive QA practices and seamlessly integrating them into the development lifecycle, organizations can foster innovation and customer satisfaction. As software systems continue to evolve in complexity and scale, the principles of Shift-Left Testing offer a practical approach to achieving sustainable quality assurance outcomes.

In conclusion, the integration of Shift-Left Testing as an advanced quality assurance technique highlights its transformative impact on software development practices. By prioritizing early intervention, automation, and collaborative synergy, organizations can effectively navigate the complexities of modern software ecosystems while delivering significant value to end-users.

Shift-Right Testing

The evolution of testing methodologies has been pivotal in meeting the escalating demands of modern software development. Among these methodologies, "Shift-Right Testing" has emerged as a strategic approach to enhance QA effectiveness and efficiency. Unlike traditional methods that mainly focus on early-stage defect prevention, Shift-Right Testing takes a proactive stance towards detecting and rectifying issues in the later stages of software development and deployment cycles.

Understanding Shift-Right Testing

Shift-Right Testing gets its name from shifting the focus of testing activities towards the later stages of the software development lifecycle (SDLC), particularly after deployment. This approach contrasts with traditional "Shift-Left" testing, which emphasizes early testing phases like unit testing and integration testing. Shift-Right Testing recognizes that despite rigorous testing efforts early in the SDLC, certain defects and vulnerabilities may go unnoticed until the software is deployed in a real-world environment.

Key Principles and Strategies

Continuous Monitoring and Feedback Loops

At the core of Shift-Right Testing is continuous monitoring and feedback loops. This involves deploying monitoring tools and techniques that actively track the performance, behavior, and usage patterns of the software in production. By collecting and analyzing real-time data, QA teams can swiftly identify anomalies, performance bottlenecks, and potential security breaches that traditional pre-deployment testing might have missed.

A/B Testing and Canary Releases

Another significant aspect of Shift-Right Testing is the adoption of A/B testing and canary releases. These techniques involve releasing new features or updates to a subset of users or servers while monitoring their impact on performance and user experience. By gradually expanding the release based on observed results, QA teams can mitigate risks associated with broader deployments and ensure smooth user experiences across diverse environments.

Chaos Engineering and Resilience Testing

In pursuit of robust software resilience, Shift-Right Testing integrates principles from chaos engineering. This involves intentionally injecting faults and failures into the production environment to assess how well the system withstands unexpected disruptions. By simulating real-world scenarios, QA teams can uncover vulnerabilities, refine fault tolerance mechanisms, and strengthen the software's overall resilience against unforeseen challenges.

Tools and Technologies

Shift-Right Testing relies on a range of advanced tools and technologies tailored to monitor, analyze, and optimize software performance in real-time. These include:

- **Monitoring Tools**: Such as Prometheus, Grafana, and ELK Stack, which provide comprehensive insights into system metrics, logs, and performance indicators.
- **Deployment Orchestration**: Platforms like Kubernetes and Docker Swarm facilitate seamless deployment and scaling of containerized applications, ensuring consistency and reliability across diverse environments.
- **Security Testing Frameworks**: Tools such as OWASP ZAP and Burp Suite enable continuous security testing to identify and mitigate vulnerabilities, thereby

strengthening the software's defense against cyber threats.

Benefits and Challenges

Benefits

- **Enhanced Bug Detection**: By focusing on real-world usage scenarios, Shift-Right Testing enhances the detection of elusive bugs and performance bottlenecks that may only emerge under specific conditions.
- **Improved User Experience**: Continuous monitoring and feedback loops enable proactive identification and resolution of issues, thereby enhancing overall user satisfaction and retention rates.
- **Agility and Iterative Improvement**: The iterative nature of Shift-Right Testing promotes agility in software development, allowing teams to iterate rapidly based on real-time feedback and market demands.

Challenges

- **Complexity**: Implementing Shift-Right Testing requires a sophisticated infrastructure and specialized expertise to manage the complexities of real-time monitoring and fault injection.
- **Resource Intensiveness**: Continuous monitoring and testing can impose significant resource demands, including computational power, storage, and human capital, necessitating careful resource allocation and optimization.

Shift-Right Testing represents a paradigm shift in software QA, emphasizing proactive detection and resolution of issues in real-world environments. By embracing continuous monitoring, A/B testing, and resilience engineering principles, organizations can elevate their QA practices to ensure robust, resilient, and user-centric software solutions. As software systems grow in complexity and scale, the adoption of Shift-Right Testing is poised to become essential in safeguarding quality and reliability across the software development lifecycle.

Chaos Engineering

Ensuring robust and resilient systems is crucial as technology evolves and digital infrastructures grow more complex. Chaos Engineering emerges as a pivotal practice in this pursuit. Unlike traditional QA methods that focus on predictable scenarios, Chaos Engineering intentionally introduces controlled disruptions to uncover vulnerabilities and improve system reliability.

Understanding Chaos Engineering

Chaos Engineering isn't about causing chaos for its own sake but systematically testing systems under realistic stress conditions. Originating from practices pioneered by Netflix, it has become a methodology adopted by leading tech firms worldwide. The goal is to proactively identify weaknesses in distributed systems before they impact production environments, minimizing downtime and enhancing user experience.

Key Principles and Methodologies

Central to Chaos Engineering are key principles guiding its implementation. Controlled experimentation is crucial: teams design experiments simulating real-world failures (like network outages or server crashes) to observe system responses. These experiments occur during off-peak hours to minimize user impact.

Another critical principle is automation. Given the scale and complexity of modern software systems, manual testing alone is insufficient. Automation allows QA teams to continuously execute chaos experiments, collect data, and analyze results systematically. This iterative process fosters continuous improvement, with each experiment informing refinements to system resilience.

Tools and Technologies

Chaos Engineering employs various tools and technologies to orchestrate experiments effectively. For instance, Netflix's Chaos Monkey randomly terminates virtual machine instances to ensure other instances can compensate seamlessly. Platforms like Gremlin and ChaosIQ enable teams to design, deploy, and analyze chaos experiments across different stack layers, from infrastructure to application components.

Benefits and Business Impact

Chaos Engineering offers tangible benefits across software development and deployment. Technically, it identifies and addresses hidden vulnerabilities overlooked by traditional testing, preemptively mitigating potential failures in production. Moreover, by enhancing system reliability and availability, organizations improve user experience, maintain customer trust, and reduce financial risks associated with downtime.

Challenges and Considerations

Implementing Chaos Engineering presents challenges. Defining meaningful chaos experiments that reflect real-world conditions without causing undue disruption requires careful planning and stakeholder communication. Effective Chaos Engineering demands cross-functional collaboration among development, operations, and QA teams to understand system dependencies and failure modes.

Future Directions and Emerging Trends

Looking ahead, Chaos Engineering evolves with advancements in cloud computing, microservices architecture, and AI. As software systems grow more distributed and dynamic, resilient design principles become more critical. Trends include integrating Chaos Engineering into DevOps pipelines for automated chaos experiments within CI/CD workflows. Additionally, AI-driven algorithms enhance the precision and scope of chaos experiments, safeguarding digital ecosystems against evolving threats.

In conclusion, Chaos Engineering represents a shift in software QA toward proactive resilience testing. By using controlled disruptions to enhance system reliability, organizations fortify digital infrastructures against unforeseen disruptions, delivering superior user experiences. As technology advances, Chaos Engineering will continue shaping software QA, ensuring systems withstand evolving challenges.

Machine Learning in Testing

There's a noticeable shift happening towards integrating advanced techniques like machine learning (ML). This shift represents a significant advancement in how the industry approaches ensuring software reliability, functionality, and performance.

Understanding Machine Learning in Testing

Machine learning, a subset of artificial intelligence (AI), has garnered considerable attention for its ability to autonomously learn patterns and behaviors from data. This capability allows systems to make predictions or decisions without explicit programming. In software QA, ML plays a crucial role in enhancing testing processes through intelligent automation and predictive analytics.

Enhancing Test Automation

One of the primary applications of ML in QA is enhancing test automation. Traditional test automation frameworks rely on predefined scripts that dictate expected behaviors and outcomes. While effective, these scripts can become fragile and require frequent updates as software evolves. ML introduces a new approach by enabling systems to learn from test results, adapt to changes in the application being tested, and adjust test cases based on real-time feedback.

ML algorithms analyze historical test data to identify patterns of success or failure, optimize test coverage, and prioritize test cases based on their likelihood of uncovering critical defects.

This capability accelerates testing and improves its effectiveness by focusing resources on areas most susceptible to errors.

Predictive Analytics for Quality Assurance

Beyond automation, ML empowers QA teams with predictive analytics. By analyzing metrics such as code complexity, historical defect data, and usage patterns, ML models can predict potential areas of risk within the software. This proactive approach allows QA professionals to allocate resources preemptively to mitigate identified risks, thereby enhancing overall product quality and reliability.

Additionally, ML-driven predictive analytics enables proactive maintenance of test environments and infrastructure. By forecasting potential performance bottlenecks or resource constraints, QA teams can scale infrastructure or optimize configurations ahead of time to maintain testing efficiency and accuracy.

Intelligent Test Case Generation

ML techniques also transform test case generation. Creating comprehensive test cases traditionally requires substantial human effort and domain expertise. ML algorithms automate test case generation by analyzing application code, user workflows, and historical defect data.

These generated test cases are not only comprehensive but also adaptive, evolving alongside changes in the software under test. Moreover, ML can simulate real-world usage scenarios and edge cases that are challenging to replicate manually, thus enhancing test coverage and revealing latent defects before they impact end-users.

Challenges and Considerations

Integrating ML into QA practices presents challenges despite its potential benefits. ML models require large volumes of high-quality data to deliver reliable predictions and insights. Ensuring the integrity and relevance of training data is crucial for the success of ML-driven QA initiatives.

Furthermore, the interpretability of ML models remains a concern. Unlike traditional testing methods where test results are straightforwardly traceable to specific test cases, insights from ML may lack transparency. QA teams must invest in tools and techniques to interpret and validate ML outputs, ensuring confidence in decision-making processes.

Additionally, as software development evolves continuously, ML models must undergo regular retraining and recalibration to maintain accuracy. This iterative process requires collaboration between QA professionals, data scientists, and software developers to align ML initiatives with evolving business needs and technological advancements.

Future Outlook

Looking ahead, the intersection of machine learning and quality assurance promises significant innovation in software engineering. As ML algorithms become more advanced and accessible, QA teams can leverage these advancements to drive efficiencies, improve software quality, and accelerate time-to-market without compromising reliability.

In summary, while adopting ML in software QA presents challenges, its transformative potential to optimize testing processes, predict defects proactively, and enhance overall software quality underscores its importance as a cornerstone of next-generation QA strategies. Embracing ML-driven QA initiatives promises to redefine industry standards and foster innovation in software development and quality assurance.

Conclusions

This advanced handbook for intermediate professionals in Software Quality Assurance (QA) Engineering has explored a range of topics essential for mastering the intricacies of modern software development and testing. From foundational principles to cutting-edge techniques, this book aims to equip QA engineers with the knowledge and skills needed to excel in their roles and contribute effectively to their organizations.

Summary of Advanced Topics

Throughout this book, we have covered advanced topics that extend beyond fundamental QA practices:

- **Test Automation Strategies**: Discussing frameworks, tools, and best practices for developing reliable automated tests that enhance efficiency.
- **Performance Testing**: Exploring methodologies to assess software performance under different loads, ensuring scalability and optimal user experience.
- **Security Testing**: Examining techniques for identifying vulnerabilities and ensuring software systems are resilient against cyber threats.
- **CI/CD Integration**: Detailing how QA processes integrate into Continuous Integration and Continuous Delivery pipelines to achieve quicker release cycles with high quality.
- **Advanced Testing Techniques**: Including exploratory testing, usability testing, and compatibility

testing, emphasizing comprehensive approaches to meet both functional and non-functional requirements.

Continuing Professional Development

In an industry that constantly evolves, ongoing learning and professional growth are essential for QA engineers. Keeping up with emerging technologies, methodologies, and industry trends is vital. Pursuing certifications, attending conferences, and engaging with peers can enrich knowledge and broaden perspectives, enabling QA engineers to adapt and thrive in dynamic environments.

Future Trends in Software QA

Looking forward, several trends are set to shape the future of Software QA:

- **AI and Machine Learning in Testing**: Automating test case generation, leveraging predictive analytics for defect prevention, and enhancing test execution efficiency.
- **Shift-Left Testing**: Integrating QA activities earlier in the development lifecycle to detect defects earlier and enhance product quality.
- **DevOps and Agile Practices**: Fostering collaboration across development, testing, and operations to accelerate software delivery.
- **Quality Engineering**: Evolving towards a holistic approach where QA is integrated throughout the development process, emphasizing quality ownership by all stakeholders.

Closing Remarks

In conclusion, excelling in Software QA Engineering demands not only technical expertise but also a commitment to continuous improvement and adaptation. This handbook aims to empower intermediate professionals with practical insights and strategies to navigate their roles effectively. By embracing the principles and practices outlined here, QA engineers can elevate their contributions, drive quality-focused outcomes, and establish themselves as indispensable assets in the software development landscape.

As you embark on your path as a Software QA Engineer, remember that excellence in QA goes beyond bug detection—it ensures software reliability, security, and alignment with user expectations. Embrace challenges as opportunities for growth, remain curious, and continually refine your skills to lead towards a future where quality is synonymous with success.

Printed in Great Britain
by Amazon

46753534R00126